All-season, all-weather fun with
sun, sand, water, wind, and snow.
More than 100 imaginative activities
all tested by kids!

THE INCREDIBLE
YEAR-ROUND
PLAYBOOK

THE YEAR-ROUND

by Elin McCoy

Random House  **New York**

Copyright © 1979 by Elin McCoy. Illustrations Copyright © 1979 by Irene Trivas.
All rights reserved under International and Pan-American Copyright Conventions.
Published in the United States by Random House, Inc., New York, and simultaneously
in Canada by Random House of Canada Limited, Toronto.

Library of Congress Cataloging in Publication Data
McCoy, Elin. The incredible year-round playbook.
SUMMARY: Presents games, projects, magic tricks, facts and figures, recipes,
experiments, crafts, and activities for use indoors and out during all seasons
and involving sun, sand, water, wind, and snow. 1. Creative activities and seat work—
Juvenile literature. 2. Games—Juvenile literature. 3. Amusements—Juvenile
literature. [1. Amusements] I. Trivas, Irene. II. Title. GV1203.M28
790.19'22 78-55909 ISBN 0-394-83564-6 pbk. ISBN 0-394-93564-0 lib. bdg.

Cover design by Bruce McGowin. Manufactured in the United States of America.
1 2 3 4 5 6 7 8 9 0

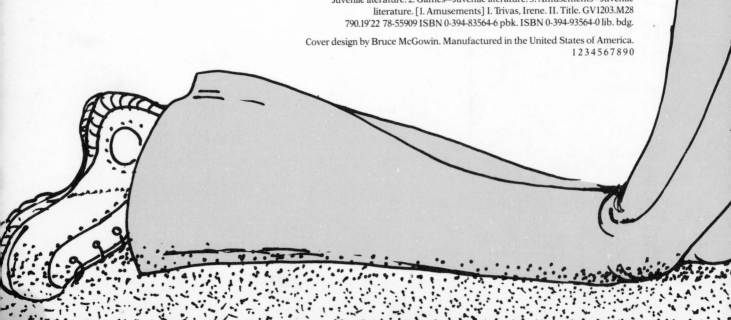

INCREDIBLE PLAYBOOK

illustrated by Irene Trivas

For Baby Griswold

Author's Acknowledgments

Many thanks to all the kids and grown-ups who tried the activities that ended up in this book, read the manuscript, or made suggestions, especially: Rebecca Elfant and kids in her classes at the Ethical Culture School in New York City, Dr. Alan J. Friedman of the Lawrence Hall of Science, Ellen Keller, Mac McCoy, Ann Morris, Tyler Norman, Aaron Shocket, Bill Walker, Casey Walker, Christy Walker, kids at Greengate Junior School in London and Riverside School in New York City, and my editor, Jenny Frisse.

An additional thank-you to Irene Trivas for her terrific illustrations.

And special thanks to John for ideas, research, advice, and general support.

About the Author and Illustrator

Elin McCoy is the author of a reading program for young children used in schools across the country. She started collecting the ideas in this book while teaching in England, added some more while teaching in the United States, and has had fun trying them out on kids from 4 to 40. Ms. McCoy has written articles and books on a wide variety of subjects, from archaeology to wine. She lives in New York City when she's writing and likes to travel and hike when she's not.

Irene Trivas has previously illustrated numerous books and educational materials. Her lively illustrations owe much to her long experience with film animation. She created the animated sequence for *Antonia* and was co-designer on *Enter Hamlet*, a short that won a prize at the Venice Film Festival. Ms. Trivas lives in East Topsham, Vermont.

Contents

Sunplay

Sandplay

Contents (continued)

Sidewalk Shadow Monsters

What lies flat on the ground, takes two or three kids to make, and will scare the dickens out of your little brother? A sidewalk shadow monster. Get some friends to help you make these on a sunny day. You'll get the biggest, scariest shadows in the early morning or late afternoon.

Three-Headed Giant Bug

Three kids stand in a line, one behind the other, with their backs to the sun. The first two hold their heads to either side and stretch out their arms to make four arm shadows. The third kid stands straight and stretches up his or her arms to make shadow antennae. Now make giant bug noises. To give your monster more arms and heads, add more kids.

Loch Ness Monster

Two, three, four, or more kids crouch on their hands and knees, one behind the other, with their sides to the sun. Another kid stands in front of them, waving his or her arms and swaying back and forth.

Shadow Shows

Give your fingers a workout with a shadow show. Go outside in the early morning or late afternoon when shadows are longest. Find a sunny wall, or hang up an old sheet on a clothesline so that the sun shines on it. Stand in front of the wall or sheet with your side to the sun and hold out your hands and arms to make some animal shadows.

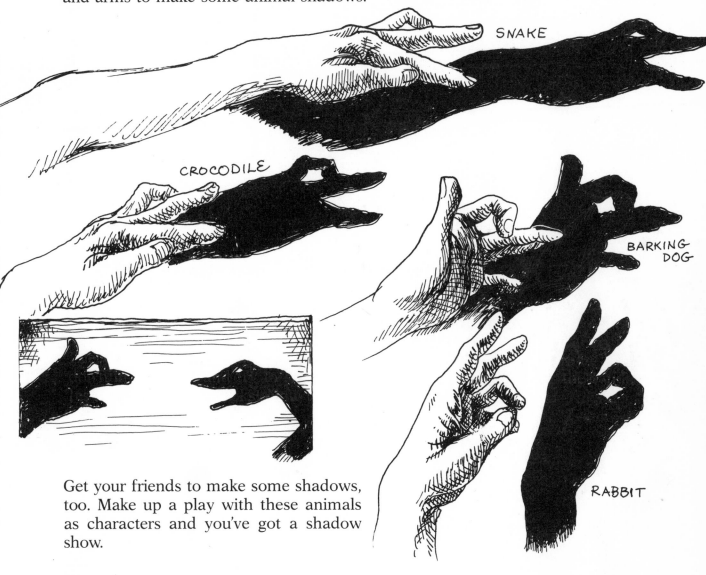

Get your friends to make some shadows, too. Make up a play with these animals as characters and you've got a shadow show.

Shadow Tag

Play this game with five or more friends on a sunny playground area or driveway. The kid picked to be *It* chases the other players, trying to step on their shadows. When *It* steps on someone's shadow, *It* shouts "Stop!" The player whose shadow is stepped on is now *It*, but he or she must stand still for three counts before chasing the other players.

Solar Energy Collecting Experiment

Did you know some colors catch more energy from sunlight than others? Try this experiment to find out which color water heater collects the most solar energy and heats water best. Watch solar energy at work!

You need three tin cans the same size and two colors of paint—black and white. Use thick poster paint, latex paint, or spray paint. You also need some water and a room thermometer.

Wash the cans and remove the labels. After you dry the cans thoroughly, paint the outside of one can black and another can white. Don't paint the third can at all. Pour the same amount of water in each can. Then set all the cans in a spot where direct sunlight hits them, such as a sunny window sill. After three hours, check the temperature of the water in each can. Keep the thermometer in each can about three minutes to get an accurate water-temperature reading. Which can is the best water heater?

Try another solar energy experiment. Get two tin cans that are the same size. Paint them black. Pour the same amount of water in each can. Cover the top of *one* can with plastic wrap. Then put the cans in sunlight. Which can is the best water heater?

Sun Power: Sun-Dried Fruit Leather

With a little help from you, sun power will dry fruit into tasty, natural snacks that will last for months. Start this project on a dry, sunny day. You'll need:

> about 1½ pounds (.7 kilograms) of very ripe peaches, plums, apricots, or strawberries
> cheesecloth (You can buy this in a dime store.)
> plastic food wrap and tape

Follow these steps:
■ Wash the fruit. Remove the stems. Peel the fruits that have skins and remove their pits. Slice the fruit.
■ Put the fruit through a food mill, blender, or food processor to turn it into a thick purée (a smooth mush). Be careful using electric appliances. Get help if you need it.
■ Heat the fruit purée in a pot over medium heat until it is almost boiling. Stir the purée often while it heats up. If it starts to stick to the bottom of the pot, add several spoonfuls of water. (Ask for help if you're not allowed to use the stove by yourself.)
■ Let the purée cool until it's lukewarm. Meanwhile cover three dinner plates with plastic food wrap. Tape the plastic to the back of the plates to keep it in place. (Instead of plates, you could cover a big bread board or a cookie sheet with plastic wrap.)
■ Pour enough fruit purée on each plate to make a thin layer about ⅛ to ¼ inch (5 centimeters) thick.
■ Place the plates inside a large roasting pan (or a shallow box). Stretch cheesecloth over the pan and tape it to the outside. (This will keep insects from getting on the purée.)
■ Put the pan outside in the sun and leave it there all day. Bring the purée inside when the sun goes down. Keep it in a dry place overnight. *Don't* put the purée in the refrigerator. It will take one to three days for the purée to dry into fruit leather. When it feels firm and peels up from the plastic wrap without sticking, it's ready to eat like candy. Don't overdry it.
■ Roll up the fruit leather in the plastic wrap. Keep it in a jar or in the refrigerator. Tear off a chunk when you feel like having a snack.

Hint: The purée won't dry properly in damp weather, so if it starts to rain, finish drying the purée in the oven. Just put the plates in an oven set on "warm" (usually the lowest heat) and leave the oven door open. Check often to see whether the purée is dry enough. (You won't need the pan and the cheesecloth for oven-drying.)

Sun Scorcher Tricks

A magnifying glass + you + a bright sun = some really hot tricks!

Paper Scorcher

Put a piece of paper on the sidewalk or in a metal pan. Put a stone on one end of the paper to keep it from blowing away. Hold a magnifying glass so that the sun shines through it and makes a small dot of light on the paper. Move the glass up and down slowly until the light makes the smallest and brightest dot. Then hold the glass steady and see how long it takes to burn a hole in the paper. Colored paper burns faster than white paper.

Hints: The dot gets *very* bright, so you might want to wear sunglasses. And *don't* try this trick in a forest or near lots of trash or in any other place where you might start a fire.

Sun Brands

When you're an old hand at scorching paper, try scorching your initials or a picture in a small block of wood. Keep the dot of sunlight the same size as you *very slowly* move it across the wood. Be patient! This takes time.

Sun Burst

Bet your friends that you can burst a balloon without touching it. Blow up a balloon and tie its neck. Then tape or tie the neck to a fence, picnic table, or post. Hold your magnifying glass to make a steady burning dot of sunlight on the surface of the balloon. Pow! You've won your bet!

Balloon-Bursting Race

Now that your friends know how to burst balloons with the sun, have a race. Each kid needs three balloons and a magnifying glass. Blow up all the balloons to the same size, tie their necks, and tape or tack them to a wall or big pieces of cardboard. Get your magnifying glasses ready, get set, go! The first kid to burst all three balloons wins the race.

Hint: The bigger the magnifying glass, the hotter it burns. But no matter what size your magnifying glass is, the most important thing is to keep the burning dot small and steady.

Sun Viewer

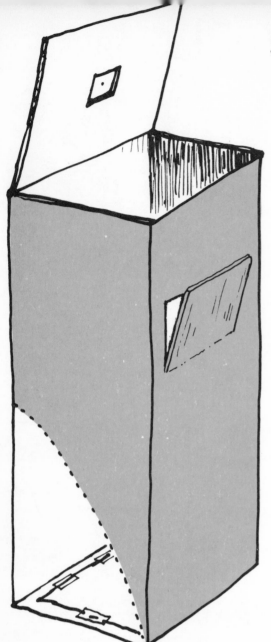

You can hurt your eyes by looking directly at the sun. But if you use this sun viewer, you can safely watch the sun, search for sunspots, and look at the next solar eclipse. You need:

> a cardboard carton at least 18 inches (45 centimeters) tall or wide, with no sides missing
> a sheet of white paper big enough to cover the smallest side of the box
> a sharp knife or carton cutter (Be careful when you use it!)
> tape, aluminum foil, a small needle

Stand the carton so that it's taller than it is wide. (If the top of your box has been cut in half, tape it shut and use the other end as the top.) Cut the top of the box along three edges to make a big flap. Tape shut any other sides that are open.

Now cut a square hole 2 inches (5 centimeters) on each side in the middle of the top. Tape a piece of smooth aluminum foil over the hole. Gently stick the needle through the center of the foil to make a *very tiny round* hole.

Cut a window flap about 6 inches (15 centimeters) wide and 4 inches (10 centimeters) high in front near the top.

Tape the paper on the bottom inside. Tape the top of the box shut.

Take the sun viewer outside when it's sunny. Set the box in the sun on the ground or a table. Pull down the flap and look down through the window at the white paper inside. Do you see a bright dot of light on it? If you don't, tilt the top of the box toward the sun.

The bright dot you see isn't just a spot of light. The sun's rays passing through the needle hole create a tiny image of the entire sun on the paper. Look for wisps of clouds passing across the sun's image and watch the image move slowly across the paper as the day goes by. If you're very lucky, you may see little dark spots on the sun's face. These sunspots are giant storms on the sun's burning surface!

Super Sun Facts

Believe it or not . . .

The sun is our nearest star, but it's still 93 million miles (150 million kilometers) away.

The sun is as big as a million earths put together.

The temperature on the surface of the sun is 11,000° Fahrenheit (6,000° Celsius)! And in the center of the sun, the temperature is 100,000,000°F (56,000,000°C)!

The sun has been burning itself up for about five billion years, and it's still got billions of years to go.

How to Measure with the Sun

Astonish friends with your ability to figure out the height of trees, buildings, and flagpoles! You'll need two one-foot rulers and a sunny day. Near a tree you want to measure, stand one ruler straight up on the ground so it casts a shadow. Measure how many *inches* long the shadow is. Then measure how many *feet* long the tree's shadow is.

Now the "trick" to finding the height of the tree is just simple arithmetic. Multiply the length of the tree's shadow by 12. Divide the number you get by the length of the ruler's shadow. The answer tells you how tall the tree is in feet. You can measure a building or a flagpole or even a friend the same way.

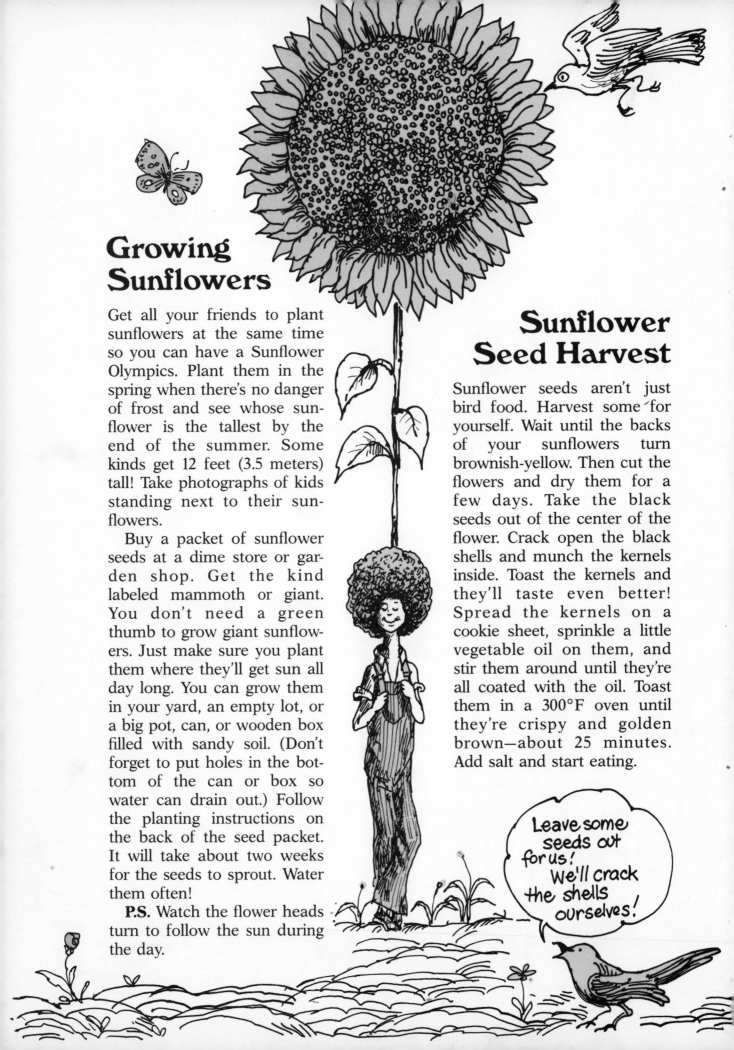

Growing Sunflowers

Get all your friends to plant sunflowers at the same time so you can have a Sunflower Olympics. Plant them in the spring when there's no danger of frost and see whose sunflower is the tallest by the end of the summer. Some kinds get 12 feet (3.5 meters) tall! Take photographs of kids standing next to their sunflowers.

Buy a packet of sunflower seeds at a dime store or garden shop. Get the kind labeled mammoth or giant. You don't need a green thumb to grow giant sunflowers. Just make sure you plant them where they'll get sun all day long. You can grow them in your yard, an empty lot, or a big pot, can, or wooden box filled with sandy soil. (Don't forget to put holes in the bottom of the can or box so water can drain out.) Follow the planting instructions on the back of the seed packet. It will take about two weeks for the seeds to sprout. Water them often!

P.S. Watch the flower heads turn to follow the sun during the day.

Sunflower Seed Harvest

Sunflower seeds aren't just bird food. Harvest some for yourself. Wait until the backs of your sunflowers turn brownish-yellow. Then cut the flowers and dry them for a few days. Take the black seeds out of the center of the flower. Crack open the black shells and munch the kernels inside. Toast the kernels and they'll taste even better! Spread the kernels on a cookie sheet, sprinkle a little vegetable oil on them, and stir them around until they're all coated with the oil. Toast them in a 300°F oven until they're crispy and golden brown—about 25 minutes. Add salt and start eating.

Leave some seeds out for us! We'll crack the shells ourselves!

The Sun-Seeking-Sweet-Potato-in-the-Shoebox Experiment

If you can say that, you can say phototropism (foe-ТОТ-ruh-piz-em). What's phototropism? Well, when plants grow toward the sun, that's called phototropism—and that's what this experiment is all about. Everybody knows plants like sunlight. But did you know that they can find it even if there's something in the way? To prove it you need:

- a shoebox
- a sprouting sweet potato planted in a small pot that will fit in the shoebox
- a piece of cardboard about the same size as the end of the shoebox
- a toilet-paper tube, scissors, and tape

Cut a hole in one end of the shoebox. Push the toilet-paper tube partway through it so the tube is sticking into the box. Tape it in place. Put the pot with the sprouting sweet potato at the end of the box farthest from the hole. Cut the piece of cardboard so that it is 1 inch (2.5 centimeters) shorter than the height of the box and 2 inches (5 centimeters) shorter than the width of the box. Tape the cardboard inside the box so the finished box looks like the one below.

Put the lid on the box. Place the box so the hole faces a window with sun. Don't take the lid off except for a few minutes when you water the plant every few days. Then you can check to see what the plant is doing to get light.

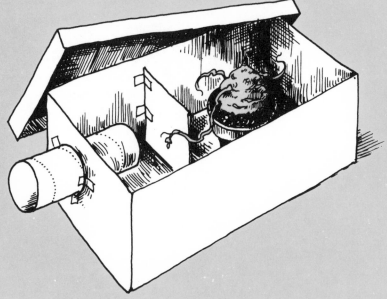

How to sprout a sweet potato: Get a very small sweet potato with little buds or "eyes" on it. Stick in three toothpicks around the middle of the potato. Put one end in a small jar of water with the toothpicks resting on the jar's edge. Keep the jar in a warm spot away from direct sunlight. Change the water in the jar every few days. After two or three weeks, the sweet potato will grow roots and then a few leaves. Plant the sprouting potato in a tiny pot filled with damp, sandy soil.

Rainbow Reflector

Make rainbows indoors on a sunny day (no rain needed!). Here's how:

Look for a window with the sun shining through it. On a table or window sill in front of it, place an ice cube tray nearly filled with water. (A shallow bowl, a cake pan or roasting pan, or a soup plate will work, too.)

Put a small pocket mirror in one end of the tray. Slowly keep changing the tilt of the mirror until it catches the sunlight and reflects colors on the wall.

Let the water become still so that the rainbow of colors doesn't wiggle. You may have to shift the position of the tray to see the rainbow at its best.

First try making a small rainbow on a wall close to your rainbow reflector. The smaller your rainbow is, the sharper and brighter the colors in it will be. Now make a big rainbow on a wall that's farther away. What happens to the colors? If your walls are a dark color, you'll have to prop a piece of white cardboard against one to see the rainbow.

P.S. You see these colors because sunlight is actually made up of every color. It just looks white most of the time. Your rainbow reflector spreads out the light and separates it into colors, the same way a prism does.

Sun-Powered Light Show

For this light show you turn off the lights. In fact, for the best results, you also fix the shades or drapes, so that only one wide bar of sunlight comes into the room. Hold mirrors, aluminum foil, light mobiles, and other reflectors in the sun and watch the light patterns on the walls and ceiling.

Hint: If your walls are dark-colored, pin or tape an old white sheet on one wall to catch the reflections.

Try these reflectors: ☀Wiggle small, smooth sheets of foil to create light waves. ☀Twist pieces of mylar to make strange light shapes. (Mylar is a thin, silvery plastic that you can buy at art supply stores and hobby shops.) ☀Flash spots of light from pocket mirrors and curved make-up mirrors. ☀Put some rainbow reflectors on the window sill. ☀Hang up a light mobile. To make: Attach two wire hangers to the bottom of a third hanger with garbage-bag ties. Cut strips of mylar, foil, or colored cellophane and tape them to the hangers. Tie a string to the hook of the top hanger so you can hang up the mobile. Hang it low enough for the sunlight to hit it. If there isn't enough breeze to turn the mobile, give it a nudge.

Sun Spot Tag

Three or four kids can play this game outdoors on a bright day. You need a small pocket mirror for each player and a wall. Hold your mirror so it reflects a spot of sunlight on the wall. Practice wiggling the mirror to move your spot around. After everyone has practiced, choose one kid to be *It*. *It* chases the other players' sun spots on the wall with his or her spot. When *It*'s spot touches another player's spot, that player becomes *It*. Let two areas on the wall be safe zones where spots can rest without being tagged. But don't let them rest too long! A spot shouldn't be allowed to stay in the safe zone for more than ten counts.

P.S. This game works best on a wall with some shadows on it.

Secret Sun Messages and Signals

Spies explorers, and people shipwrecked on desert islands have used mirrors and the sun to send messages or to signal for help. By letting the sun's rays bounce off their mirrors, they make bright flashes that other people can see from far away. They sometimes set up secret codes in which a certain number of flashes means a certain word or message. You can do your own sun signaling with a friend. On a sunny day, get a pocket mirror and a piece of cardboard (bigger than the mirror) for each person. Decide on a secret code of flashes like the one below, and you're all set.

Catch the sunlight on your mirror. Hold it to reflect a spot of light on the ground or a wall. Then carefully move the mirror to aim the spot of light at your friend. (It will be easiest to send a message if you're facing the sun or if the sun is overhead.) You'll probably have to practice this a few times. Your friend can help you check your aim by waving when he or she sees the sun flash off your mirror.

Now brace the mirror against your body to keep the spot steady. Cover and uncover the mirror with the piece of cardboard to send the message. Each time you uncover the mirror counts as a flash. Cover the mirror and count to 3 between flashes. Count to 15 between messages. Here are some sample flash-code messages:

> two flashes = come over right away
> three flashes = meet me on the corner in ten minutes
> four flashes = can't come over, must clean my room

21

Sun Prints

Make this special kind of photograph outdoors without a camera and develop it yourself right away. Here's what you need:

- a package of studio proof paper (Buy it at a camera store. You can also use other kinds of contact printing paper, but studio proof paper works best.)
- a 6-ounce (170-gram) package of fixer (Buy this at a camera store, too.)
- a Manila envelope, at least half the size of the studio proof paper
- a 1-quart (1-liter) jar with lid
- 2 small plastic pails or pans
- a plastic spoon with a long handle
- kitchen tongs or clip clothespin
- a marking pen
- tape
- scissors
- paper towels
- a watch or clock
- water

Here's what to do:

1. In a dark room, open the package of studio proof paper, slide out two or three sheets, and close up the package. Cut the sheets in half and put them in the Manila envelope so they won't darken before you're ready.

2. Fill the quart jar with lukewarm water and pour it into one pail. Put a strip of tape on the pail and write "rinse" on it.

3. Now make the fixer. (Be careful handling it. Remember to wash your hands after you've made it.) Pour a quart of lukewarm water into the empty pail. Stir the water as you pour in the fixer powder. Keep stirring until the powder dissolves. It's okay if the mixture looks cloudy. Mark that pail "fixer." Pour about half the fixer into the quart jar and save it for making sun prints another day. It will last about two months. (Be sure to screw the lid on tight and label the jar.)

4. Take the two pails, the envelope of studio proof paper, the kitchen tongs or clothespin, the watch, and some paper towels outside.

5. You're all set to print something. Your hand is a good first choice. Quickly take out one sheet of studio proof paper, put it in the sun with the shiny side up, and place your hand on it. (Don't let your shadow fall on the paper!)

6. Keep your hand steady for about 2 minutes. You'll see the color of the paper around your hand turn a dark purplish-brown. When you lift your hand, you'll see a white print of it on the paper!

7. "Fix" the print right away to keep it from fading. Pick it up with the tongs or clothespin and dip it completely into the fixer solution. Wiggle it in the fixer for about 2 minutes. The purplish-brown will turn light brown. Leave the print in the fixer for another 2 minutes. Then take it out with the tongs.

8. Now dip the print into the "rinse." Wiggle it gently for about 2 minutes and leave it in the water for another 2 minutes or longer.

9. Put the print on a piece of paper towel in the shade to dry. Put stones on the corners to keep it flat.

Now that you know how to make a sun print, try printing leaves, shells, paper clips, keys, combs, bones, spaghetti and macaroni patterns, scissors, flowers, and anything else you want. For prints of small objects, cut sheets of studio proof paper into several small pieces. Just remember to cut them up in a dark room!

Hint: It isn't necessary to time everything exactly. If you leave the print in the sun longer, you'll just get a darker background.

Contact Camera

Use this handy contact camera when you want sun prints of flat things to have extra sharp outlines. You can even use it to make prints from black-and-white photographic negatives!

To make the camera, tape one edge of a piece of glass to one edge of a piece of cardboard. The two pieces should open and close like a book. To make a print, put a piece of studio proof paper, shiny side up, on the cardboard. Place a flat object or negative on the paper. Fold down the glass and put your camera in the sun. After two minutes, take the print out and fix it.

GLASS OR CLEAR STIFF PLASTIC WITH TAPE ON ITS EDGES

STUDIO PROOF PAPER

TAPE HINGE

CORRUGATED CARDBOARD

Sun Compass

It's nice to know that you can always find north, south, east, and west if there's enough sun to make shadows—especially if you get lost. This easy sun compass gives the most accurate directions in the middle of the day, between 11 A.M. and 1 P.M.

In a flat, sunny spot, shove a stick about three feet (one meter) long into the ground. Make sure it's standing up straight. Use a stone to mark the end of the shadow it makes.

STONE # 1.

Wait about 20 minutes. Mark the end of the shadow the stick makes now with another stone.

STONE # 2

P.S: This Compass works in the Southern Hemisphere too, but there you have to face the sun when you put your feet on the stones.

Now stand with your *back* to the sun. Put your *left* foot on the *first* stone. Put your *right* foot on the *second* stone (that's the one with the shadow on it now). You're facing north. If you stick out your arms, your left arm will point west and your right arm will point east. South is behind you.

Sun Clock

You'll never have to wind this clock—it's sun-powered! To make it, you need:

- a piece of heavy cardboard about 18 inches (45 centimeters) on each side
- an empty thread spool
- 2 pencils, one of them about 6 inches (15 centimeters) long
- tape and a ruler
- a watch or clock

Start making your sun clock first thing in the morning. Find a spot outdoors that's sunny all day. Tape the cardboard to a flat surface—a table or box—so it won't move or blow away. Tape the spool in the center of the cardboard and stick the 6-inch pencil in the spool's hole.

Now check the time. If it's 7:48, come back to your sun clock at exactly 8:00. You want to put a dot at the end of the pencil's shadow exactly on the hour and write the time next to it. Do this every hour during the day. By the end of the afternoon, you'll have dots in a curve across the cardboard.

Use a ruler to draw lines from the dots to the spool so your clock looks like the one below. Don't worry if your shortest line isn't at noon. Depending on where you live, the shortest line may be at an earlier or later time.

Put your clock in the same spot the next day. The pencil shadow will tell you what time it is. This clock says 10:30.

Hint: The only trouble with this clock is that if you move it, you have to reset it. Check the time on a watch or clock and turn the cardboard until the pencil shadow falls on that time.

Suntan Tattoos

Want a natural tattoo? All you have to do is make sure sunlight doesn't hit some areas on your skin and does hit others.

For stripes around your arms and legs, cut leg and arm bands at least one inch wide from the tops of old socks. Slide one band around each arm or leg. Wear the bands in exactly the same places each time you go out in the sun. In about a week, you'll see stripes.

For fancier tattoos, cut self-sticking labels into shapes and stick them on your arms, forehead, or back when you go out in the sun. (You can buy these labels in stationery or office supply stores.) Try wearing heart shapes, circles, squares, or your initials. Keep to big, simple shapes for best results. Remember: Stick the shapes in the same places each time you go out in the sun.

AN IMPORTANT HINT:

Don't try to hurry up the tattooing process by staying out in the sun too long—you might get sunburned and end up peeling off your tattoo!

SANDPLAY

Sand Sculpture

Mold it, drip it, carve it, pack it—with water, your hands, and a few tools, you can shape sand into practically anything.

Good things to put in your sand sculpture tool kit:

pails • bowls • paper cups • cardboard tubes
fancy molds • milk cartons • all kinds of cans
plastic food containers • coffee measurers
small boxes—from matchboxes to shoeboxes
funnels • cake pans • yardsticks and rulers
big spoons • spatulas • scoops • forks
combs • a bucket of water

Mold It

Pack wet sand into a mold. Carefully turn the mold upside down and gently lift it off. If the sand sticks to it, tap the mold lightly before you pull it off.

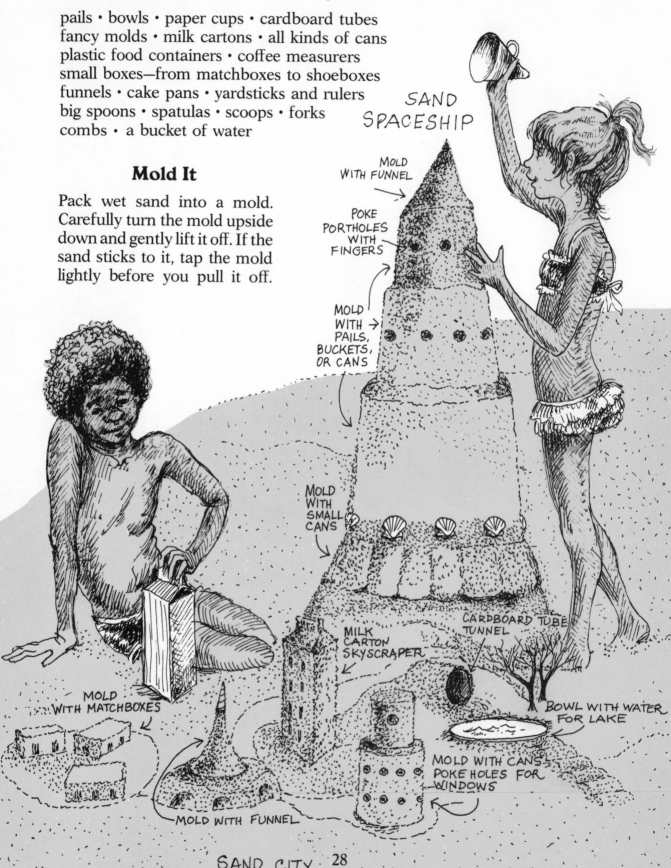

SAND SPACESHIP

MOLD WITH FUNNEL

POKE PORTHOLES WITH FINGERS

MOLD WITH PAILS, BUCKETS, OR CANS

MOLD WITH SMALL CANS

CARDBOARD TUBE TUNNEL

MILK CARTON SKYSCRAPER

BOWL WITH WATER FOR LAKE

MOLD WITH MATCHBOXES

MOLD WITH FUNNEL

MOLD WITH CANS POKE HOLES FOR WINDOWS

SAND CITY 28

Pack and Carve It

Make a pile of damp sand and pack it into a hard mound with your hands. Use spoons, rulers, yardsticks, and spatulas to carve the mound into a shape. Repack each area you scrape.

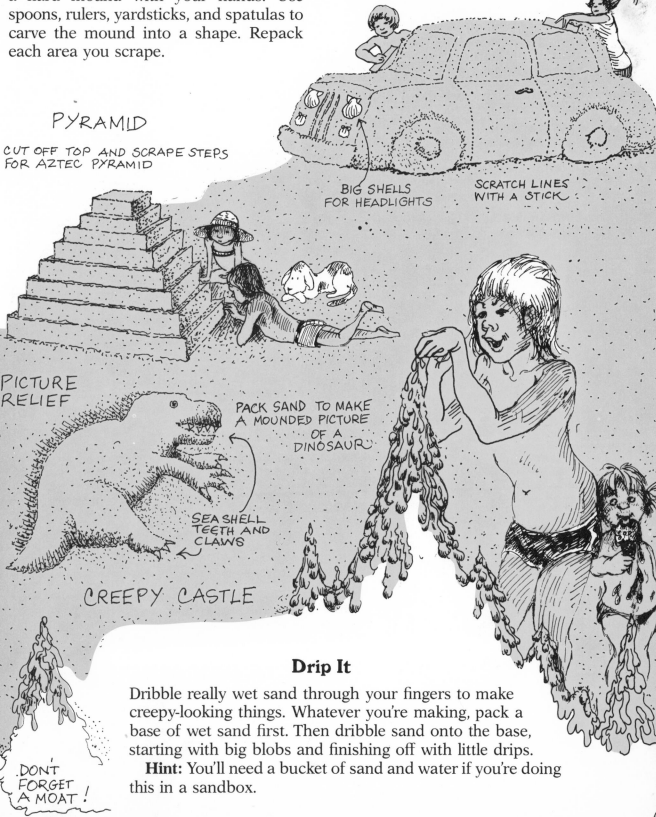

CAR (AN ALL-DAY PROJECT)

BIG SHELLS FOR HEADLIGHTS

SCRATCH LINES WITH A STICK

PYRAMID

CUT OFF TOP AND SCRAPE STEPS FOR AZTEC PYRAMID

PICTURE RELIEF

PACK SAND TO MAKE A MOUNDED PICTURE OF A DINOSAUR

SEA SHELL TEETH AND CLAWS

CREEPY CASTLE

DON'T FORGET A MOAT!

Drip It

Dribble really wet sand through your fingers to make creepy-looking things. Whatever you're making, pack a base of wet sand first. Then dribble sand onto the base, starting with big blobs and finishing off with little drips.

Hint: You'll need a bucket of sand and water if you're doing this in a sandbox.

P.S: YOU CAN MAKE ALL THESE THINGS IN MINIATURE ON A SAND SLATE. (SEE PAGE 32.)

Sand Detective

Get down to the nitty gritty and see what's in your sand. Here are four ways to test it.

Test #1: Shake It Up

Dump a handful of sand in a jar. Fill the jar up with water and screw on the lid. Shake hard. Then quickly set the jar down and watch the sand settle. If the grains of your sand are about the same size, you won't see any difference between the sand that settles on the bottom of the jar and the sand that settles on top. If the grains of sand are very different in size, you'll see several layers of sand, with grains of a different size in each layer. The big ones will fall to the bottom. The medium-sized grains will make the next layer. The very tiniest grains will be on top.

Test #2: Will It Fizz?

Dump a handful of sand in the bottom of a bowl. Pour in white vinegar until the sand is covered. If the sand-and-water mixture fizzes (you'll see tiny bubbles), then your sand has bits of limestone or broken shell in it. If there's no fizzing, it doesn't.

Test #3: Eyeball It

Put about a tablespoon of sand on a sheet of white paper. Look at the grains through a magnifying glass while you move them around with your finger or a toothpick. Are there bits of dirt, wood, or seaweed in the sand? Are the grains of sand the same color or different colors? What colors do you see?

Sand is made of tiny pieces of crushed rocks and minerals. Different rocks and minerals are different colors. The color of the grains of sand will tell you what kinds of rocks or minerals your sand came from. Lots of pink, yellow, white, or gray bits mean your sand is mostly from a mineral called feldspar. Clear, sparkly grains are quartz or mica, which are also minerals. Sometimes you'll see shiny, black grains. These are another kind of mica. Brown grains are probably from sandstone, a type of rock.

Test #4: Prospect It

Put a couple of spoonfuls of sand on a sheet of paper. Spread the sand in a thin layer. Wrap a piece of plain white paper around a magnet and slowly move it just above the spread-out sand. If little dark particles stick to the paper around the magnet, your sand contains magnetite, a type of iron ore that's magnetic. Brush the magnetite particles onto another sheet of plain paper. Hold up the paper with the magnetite and slowly pass the magnet underneath it. You'll see the magnetite particles dance!

Portable Sand Slate

Flat damp sand is great for writing messages or drawing pictures. Try sand writing and sand sketching at the beach or in a sandbox or, best of all, on a portable sand slate that you've made yourself. Find a large, shallow metal pan or cardboard carton (make sure it's made of strong, heavy cardboard). It should be at least 1 foot (30 centimeters) wide, 1½ feet (45 centimeters) long, and 3 inches (7.5 centimeters) deep. For a big portable sand slate on wheels, use an old wagon. Line your container with a sheet of plastic and then fill it with sand.

Wet the surface of the sand and smooth it with a ruler. Keep a plastic sprayer filled with water handy so you can dampen the sand whenever it gets dry.

Here's what to do with your sand slate:

Write messages, your name, or letters on it.
Draw pictures on it.
Play games like tic-tac-toe on it.
Make sand patterns and designs on it with forks, hand rakes, combs, potato mashers, and anything else you can think of.
Build miniature sand sculptures. (See page 28.)

P.S. A ruler makes a good "eraser."

Sandcast a Footprint

Do sandcasting any place there's sand—the beach, a sandbox, or on your portable sand slate. You need:

    plaster of Paris (Buy a 5-pound or 2-kilogram bag at a hardware store.)
    a large coffee can (2-pound or 1-kilogram size)
    a stick that you can throw away
    a measuring cup
    water

Dampen an area of sand that's bigger than your foot. Pack the sand down and smooth it. Make a footprint in it about 1½ inches (4 centimeters) deep. Now put 2 cups of water in the coffee can. Pour in the plaster of Paris until the hill of powder reaches just above the water. Stir it with the stick. The mixture should be about as thick as a milk shake. It will start getting hard pretty quickly, so pour it gently into the footprint right away. (You may not need to use all the plaster to fill your footprint.)

Wait an hour or so for the plaster to dry completely. It should feel cool and hard. Carefully lift your plaster footprint out of the sand and brush or rinse off the loose sand. A thin layer of sand will remain on your footprint.

Use the same method to make fossils with shells and bones, handprints, your name, crazy statues, and giant footprints.

HINT: If you cast your name, don't forget to write the letters backward and in reverse order.

PLASTER OF PARIS

Another Hint: Sometimes you'll need a wall of sand to keep the wet plaster in place.

Incredible Sand Creatures

The sand lizard is super-equipped for sand living. It has fringes of tiny, pointed scales on its toes that help it swim through the sand and up sand dunes. Flaps on its ears and nose keep sand out. Its eyelids lock together tight, like pieces of a puzzle, so sand won't get in its eyes.

The sand lizard is hard to spot and even harder to catch! It's the same color as the sandy desert where it lives, and it's only 6 inches (15 centimeters) long. Besides, it can get out of sight in a flash. When the sand lizard wants to hide, it just buries itself in the sand.

GOING   GOING...   GONE!

But keep a sharp lookout for a sand lizard if you visit a sandy desert in California, Colorado, or the southwestern states. (Sand lizards live in Australian, African, and Arabian deserts, too.) Maybe you'll be lucky enough to spot one!

A young ant lion uses sand to help it catch its favorite food—ants. This insect starts digging a funnel-shaped pit in the sand right after it hatches. (Ant lions lay their eggs in sand on beaches and deserts.) When the pit is about 2 inches (5 centimeters) deep, the ant lion buries itself at the bottom, leaving only its head and jaws sticking out. Every time an ant comes too close to the edge of this sand trap, it starts to slip down the side. The ant lion throws sand at it to make sure it falls. The unlucky ant slides right down the sand trap into the ant lion's waiting jaws! Yum!

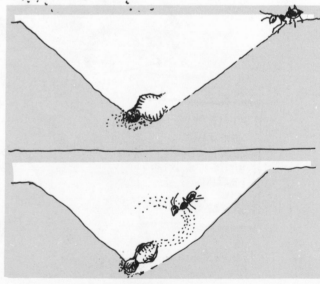

Sand-Jar Ant Ranch

Catch some ants yourself so you can watch them build tunnels in sand. You'll need:

- cheesecloth (You can buy this at a dime store.)
- 2 large glass jars with screw-on lids
- a paper-towel (or toilet-paper) tube
- a sheet of paper with a dab of honey on it
- dry sand with a little dirt mixed in

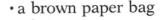

- a brown paper bag
- a hammer
- a big nail
- scissors

Cut the paper-towel tube so that it's 1 inch (2.5 centimeters) shorter than one jar. Put it in the middle of the jar and fill the space around it with sand. (The cardboard tube will keep your ants from making their tunnels in the center of the jar, where you couldn't see them.) The sand should come nearly to the top of the tube. Your jar should look like this: ⟶

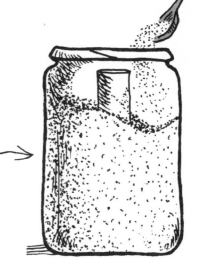

Punch a lot of small holes in the lid of the jar with the hammer and nail. Cut two squares of cheesecloth bigger than the lid. Leave the lid and the cheesecloth next to the jar while you go to find some ants.

Take the honey paper and the other jar and lid on your ant hunt. Look for ant hills or look under flat stones in your yard or in empty lots. When you find one spot with plenty of ants, put out the honey paper for bait. As the ants walk onto the paper, brush them off into the jar. Collect a few dozen—all from the same spot.

Then take the ants home and dump them into the sand jar. Quickly put the squares of cheesecloth over the top of the jar and screw on the lid. Put the paper bag over the jar (ants like to work in the dark). When you take the bag off in a day or two, you'll see the ants tunneling away! Keep the bag over the jar when you're not looking at them.

P.S. When you're tired of running an ant ranch, let the ants go—in the yard!

Ant food: bits of honey, scraps of lettuce, a couple of bread crumbs, and a few drops of water. Feed your ants once a week.

Sand Timers

Before clocks and watches were invented, people used sand timers to measure how long it took to do something. Make one yourself. Use it for timing races, contests, and boiled eggs.

Simple Sand Timer

You need:

> very fine dry sand (sift it carefully through a strainer to remove all the big particles)
> 2 small jars exactly the same size, with screw-on lids (make sure they're clean and dry)
> a sheet of heavy paper
> tape
> a watch or clock with a second hand

Make a cone out of the paper. Before you tape it, make sure there's a tiny hole in the bottom. Put the cone in the mouth of one jar. Get your watch ready. Decide how many minutes you want your timer to measure. Fill the other jar half-full of sand. Pour the sand into the cone, and start timing how long the sand takes to get through the cone into the jar. As soon as the right number of minutes has passed, pull out the cone and dump out the sand that's left in it.

Now you're ready to time something. Put the cone in the empty jar. Pour the measured sand into the cone. The time's up when all the sand has run into the jar.

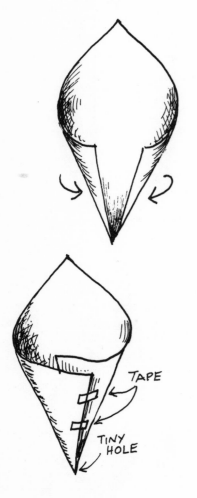

HOW TO MAKE A PAPER CONE:

BRING TWO SIDES OF THE PAPER TOGETHER SO ONE SIDE OVERLAPS THE OTHER.

TAPE

TINY HOLE

Super Sand Timer

Make your simple sand timer into a super sand timer. You just flip the super timer over whenever you want to start timing something. Get a hammer, a big nail, and some strong glue (any kind that will work on metal, like epoxy), and get started.

Step 1   Glue the lids of your two jars back to back so they look like this:
Carefully follow the directions on the tube of glue. Don't get epoxy glue on your fingers.

Step 2   Check the directions on your glue to see how long it will take to dry. When the time is up, punch holes in the lids with a hammer and a big nail. Punch them in a pattern like this: or this:

Punch about half the holes from one side, and then turn the lids over and punch half from the other side.

Step 3   Now add sand to one jar until it's half-full. Screw on the lids and then screw the other jar on top.

Step 4   Get your watch ready. Turn the timer over and start timing. See how long the sand takes to get from the top jar to the bottom jar. Add or take away sand until the timer measures the number of minutes you want.

Sand Squiggles

Squirt white glue in thin, squiggly lines on colored paper. Make swirls, write your name, draw a picture, or make a design. Sprinkle plain or colored dry sand all over the paper. Don't miss any spots. Let the glue dry until it feels hard when you touch it. Shake the loose sand off the paper, and you have a sand squiggle.

How to Color Sand

1. Put some dry sand in a jar with a screw-on lid. (If your sand is from the seashore, rinse it to get the salt out before you color it. Put the sand in a bucket. Fill the bucket with water and stir the sand around. Let the sand settle, then pour off the water. Repeat this process three times. Then spread the sand on newspaper to dry.)

2. Add several drops of food coloring to the jar. Use more if you want a darker color.

3. Screw the lid on the jar and shake the jar until the sand is completely colored.

4. Dump the sand on newspaper. Spread it around so it will dry faster. The sand will be much lighter in color when it's dry.

P.S. The handiest way to store colored sand is in clear glass jars. Keep each color in a different jar.

Recipe for a Sandpainting

What feels like sandpaper and looks like a painting? A sandpainting. The ingredients are two or more colors of sand, white glue, and a piece of cardboard. You'll also need these tools: a tin can, a small paintbrush, and a pencil.

First draw a simple design or picture on the piece of cardboard and decide which color each part will be. Don't make your picture too complicated or plan to use too many colors. In the tin can, mix a little (just a little!) water with some white glue to make it thinner. Pick one color of sand as your starting color. Brush the thinned glue on the parts of the picture that will be that color. Then sprinkle sand of that color on the glue. Let the glue dry for a few minutes. When it no longer feels sticky, shake off the extra sand. Do the same thing for each part of the painting that's a different color.

Here's a whale of a sandpainting done with four colors of sand:

Beach Hopscotch

You play hopscotch on the beach the same way you play hopscotch on the sidewalk, but it's harder to cheat. If you step on a line drawn in the sand, everybody can see your footprint!

Smooth a big area of damp sand. Draw the hopscotch squares on it with a stick. Write the numbers to the side of the squares so they won't get messed up. Use shells as tokens instead of rocks.

In case you've forgotten how to play, here's one way. Throw your token into square 1. Hop over that square into square 2, then jump into squares 3 and 4 so that one foot lands in each square. Hop and jump your way to squares 9 and 10. Jump around, hop and jump back, and hop in square 1 to pick up your token. Hop out to the starting point. Throw your token to square 2 and proceed the same way, this time hopping over square 2. If your token lands in the wrong square or you hop on a line, move your token back one square and let the next player take a turn. Remember that players have to hop over all squares that have tokens in them. The first kid to pick up a token in square 10 and hop back out wins.

Jump the River

The more kids you have for this game, the more fun it will be. Draw two lines about 1 inch (2.5 centimeters) apart in the sand to represent the "river." All the kids take turns jumping over the river. Then draw another line, making a wider river for everyone to jump over. Keep widening the river. Kids who can't jump over it are out. The one who can jump the widest river wins.

Sand Handshake

Everybody should try this at least once. You and a friend each stick an arm down in the sand and try to shake hands with one another under the sand. It's not as easy as it looks! Now try to touch toes.

Sand-Jar Art

Make empty jars worth looking at. Be a sand-jar artist. Collect or make different colors of sand (page 38 tells how), find a widemouthed jar with a lid, and get a big spoon and a small paintbrush.

Spoon sand of one color into the jar and spread it out with the paintbrush to make an even layer. On top of that, spoon sand of another color. Spread that out evenly with the brush, too. To make a jagged design, poke points from a layer of sand down into the one below with a pencil or knitting needle. Do each layer before spooning in the next one. Keep making layers of colored sand until you fill up the jar to the very top. Put on the lid. Don't shake the jar up!

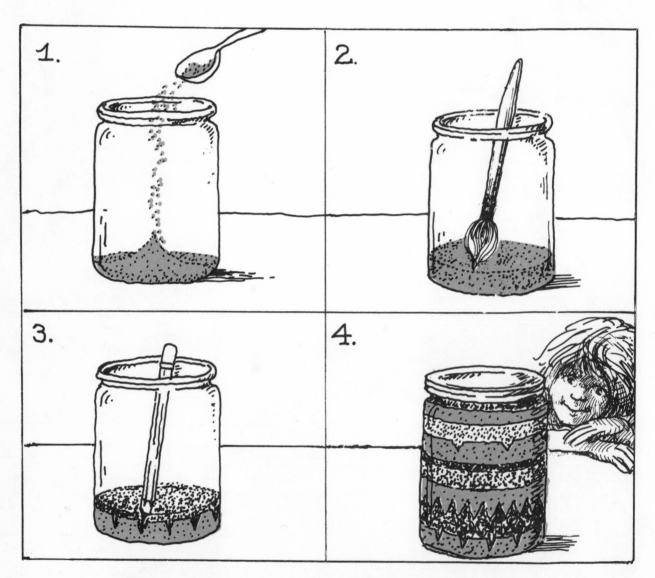

P.S. Sand jars make great bookends.

Sand Bands

Want really different bracelets, armbands, necklaces, or headbands? Make them with aquarium tubing and several colors of sand. (Page 38 tells how to color sand.) In the fish department of a pet shop or dime store, buy clear plastic flexible tubing that's ¼ inch wide.

Hold the tubing around your wrist, arm, head, or neck to see how long a piece you'll need for what you want to make. Cut off that length. Use a matchstick or a little piece of wood as a plug for one end of the tubing. Push it halfway into the tubing. If the plug doesn't fit very tightly, wrap it with tape to make it fatter.

Pouring the sand in the tubing is easier with a paper-cone funnel (page 36 shows how to make one). Pour a little sand in the cone. After it slides all the way to the bottom of the tubing and settles, carefully pour in sand of another color. Keep making layers of different colored sand until the tubing is just about filled. Push the open end of the tubing onto the plug to join the two ends together. Put on your sand band!

PLUG

Sand-Bag Lanterns

You can make lanterns to light up a summer night with sand, paper bags, and candles. First figure out how many lanterns you want. Get candles that are at least 4 inches (10 centimeters) long and medium-sized plain brown-paper grocery bags that are at least 1 foot (30 centimeters) tall. You need one bag and one candle for each lantern. Fold down the top of each bag so that it looks like this:

The candle should still be a few inches shorter than the bag. Put 3 inches (7.5 centimeters) of sand in the bottom of each bag.

Put the bags wherever you want your lanterns. Get permission to use the spot. Choose an open place outside that isn't close to anything that might catch fire. Some good places: around a patio, in the backyard, along the edge of a driveway, and at the beach.

In each bag, push a candle down in the center of the sand and pack the sand around it. Make sure it's standing up straight, won't tip easily, and is in the *middle* of the bag. Use wooden kitchen matches to light the candles. If you're not allowed to use matches, get someone older to light them for you.

These lanterns glow in the dark and won't blow over or blow out. When a candle burns down, it will put itself out in the sand. But you shouldn't leave any lanterns burning unattended.

WATERPLAY

Backyard Water Party

When it gets really hot, invite your friends over to get wet. Tell your parents your party will be a great way to water the lawn. Make sure you tell everybody to come in a bathing suit.

Make a Water Slide

Spread an old plastic shower curtain or big plastic table-cloth on the grass. Anchor the corners with stones or plastic jugs filled with water. Lay a hose at one end. Adjust the nozzle for fan spray and turn on the water. When the plastic is completely wet, jump in front of the hose nozzle and start sliding.

Have a Water War

Fill balloons and small plastic bags with water to make water bombs. Tie knots in the necks. Soak lots of sponges in buckets of water. They're super squishy throwers. Use different kinds of plastic spray bottles and basters as squirt guns. Get your weapons ready and fire away!

P.S. Pick out one area of the backyard to be a safe zone where kids can go to dry off.

Hold a Squirt-Gun Shoot-Out

Line up three bottles on a table or box for each kid. Put a ping-pong ball or empty film can on top of each bottle. Everyone stands back a yard or two. When someone shouts "Draw," the kids fire their squirt guns at their targets. The first kid to knock off all three balls or film cans wins.

Spin Water Whirlers

To make a water whirler, first make three holes near the top of a 1-quart (1-liter) yogurt or cottage cheese container. Leave about the same amount of space between the holes. Cut three pieces of string 2 feet (60 centimeters) long. Tie each piece to one hole. Make a good tight knot. Then tie the ends of the strings together. Fill your container half-full of water.

Spin your whirler around and around really fast. The water won't spill out. Try spinning it different ways. Then see how slowly you can spin the whirler without getting drenched.

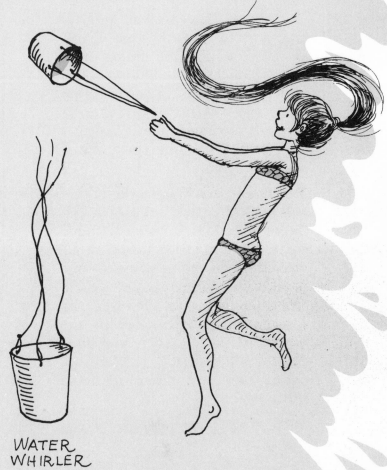

WATER WHIRLER

47

The Strange Case of the Creeping Color Dots

Are some colors hiding inside other colors? Let water squeeze out the truth. Here's how to put it to work as a color detective.

Put a little water (½ inch or 1.5 centimeters deep) in a tall glass jar. Cut three strips of paper longer than the jar from white paper toweling, coffee-filter paper, or the edge of a newspaper. Attach a paper clip to one end of each strip. Using food coloring or ink, put a tiny dot of green on one strip, purple on another, and red on the third. The dots should be about 1½ inches (4 centimeters) from the paper clips. Hang the strips of paper in the jar so the paper clips touch the water. Tape the top ends to the outside of the jar and place the jar lid on top.

You won't have to wait long for the water to crack the case. If any of the color dots are hiding other colors, you'll see the hidden colors appear when the water moves up the strips. After the water is through separating the colors in a dot, it'll even put them back together again!

P.S. The reason this works is that water moves each color at a different speed. If a color is made up of different colors (as green is), the different colors will separate from each other as they move. So when the green dot dissolves, the fast-moving yellow races to the top of the strip. When the slow-moving blue finally catches up, the two colors combine to make green again.

P.P.S. What colors were in the red and purple?

Can Shoelaces Drink Water?

The answer is yes. See if yours will by doing this experiment. Get at least three different shoelaces—a fat one, a thin one, and a medium one. Try to find at least one made from 100% cotton. Put one end of each shoelace in a bowl of water. Lay the other end of each shoelace in a separate jar lid. (All the lids should be the same size.) Keep checking the lids to see which shoelace fills a lid with water fastest.

Make an Automatic Plant Waterer

So what can you do with your thirsty shoelace? Simple. Make this automatic plant waterer. Pick out a plant growing in a small pot. Push one end of your thirstiest shoelace about 1 inch (2.5 centimeters) down in the soil and pack soil around it so it won't fall out. Fill a pint (.5 liter) jar with water and put the other end of the shoelace in it. Make sure the water level in the jar is a couple of inches higher than the pot and your shoelace will do the rest.

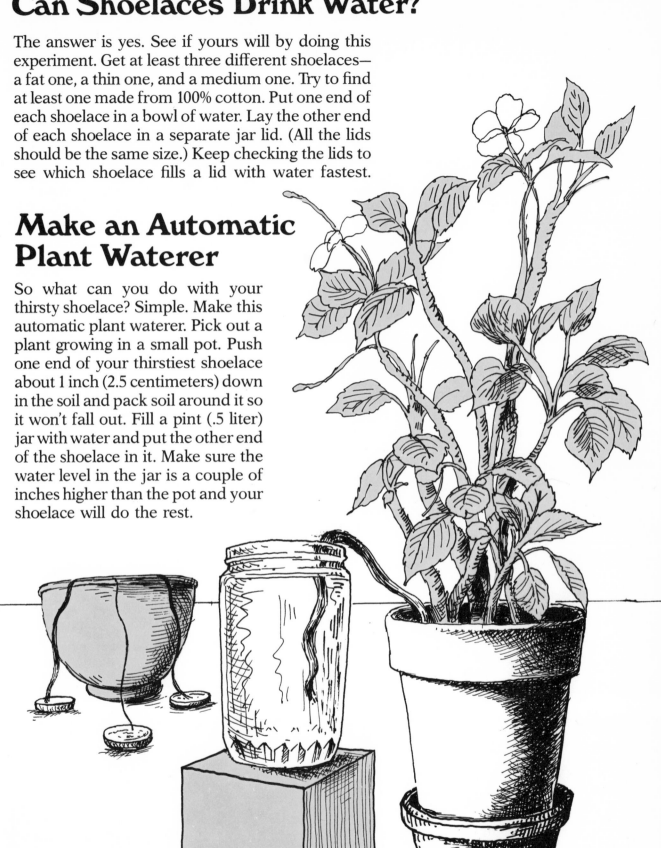

A Bunch of Boats

What's more fun than messing around with a boat? Messing around with lots of boats. Start your own mini-boatyard by building the ones below. Then just add water.

Walnut Sailboats

Press a tiny piece of clay in the bottom of half a walnut shell. Stick a toothpick into the clay for a mast. Cut a triangle of paper for the sail, punch little holes in the top and bottom of it, and slide the sail on the mast.

Balloon Jet Boat

Cut off the front side of a milk carton (the side on which the spout opens). Then staple the spout closed. Make a very small hole on the opposite side near the bottom of the carton. Stick a balloon in the carton, push the neck through the hole, and blow up the balloon. Hold the neck until you put the boat in the water. Then let go and watch the boat take off!

P.S. To keep your jet boat going longer, slow it down by twisting a plastic-bag tie around the neck of the balloon.

STAPLE
SPOUT CLOSED →

MILK

Styrofoam Trimaran

A trimaran (TRY-muh-ran) is a sailboat with three hulls. You can make one from pieces of styrofoam packing material or an old styrofoam ice chest that nobody wants. If you can't find any styrofoam around the house, you can buy pieces of it at a hobby shop.

With toothpicks, attach a narrow piece of styrofoam to each side of a larger piece of styrofoam. (If you need to cut your styrofoam into pieces, use a bread knife or a coping saw.) Push a thin stick into the large piece of styrofoam to make a mast. Cut a rectangular sail from stiff paper and make holes in the top and bottom. Slide it on the mast.

DECORATE WITH PAPER-TOWEL-TUBE SMOKESTACKS

A GOOD-SIZED PADDLE IS IMPORTANT

Mississippi Paddle Boat

Find a big, thick piece of wood (or styrofoam) for the boat and a small, thin one for the paddle. You can make a boat any size. For a medium-sized one, use a piece of wood about 4 inches (10 centimeters) wide and 8 inches (20 centimeters) long. If you want to make the wood look more like a boat, saw off two corners. Make the paddle about 1½ inches (4 centimeters) wide and 3 inches (8 centimeters) long. If you use a bigger piece of wood for the boat, you'll need a bigger piece of wood for the paddle.

Tape two tongue depressors (or popsicle sticks) securely to the boat—one to each side—so they stick out in back. Be sure to run the tape all the way around the boat. Stretch a strong rubber band around the other ends of the tongue depressors. Stick the paddle in between the two sides of the rubber band. Turn it around and around in the direction *away* from the boat, twisting the rubber band very tight. Now put your boat in the water. It's ready to roll!

Instant Water-Insect Aquarium

Water insects put on a good show. Water striders walk on water. Whirligig beetles whirl and dance, dive, and swim in circles. And back swimmers swim on their backs and use their legs like oars. Go on an insect-capturing expedition to a pond and you can bring back an aquarium.

Take:
- pieces of cheesecloth (You can buy this at a dime store.)
- a large widemouthed jar
- a plastic jug with a screw-on top
- a medium-sized plastic bowl
- a strainer
- a big spoon
- a big rubber band

Scoop up enough sand or mud from the edge of the pond to make a layer 1 inch (2.5 centimeters) deep in the jar. Dig up two or three tiny plants and plant them in the jar. Press pebbles around their roots to keep them in place. Then dip the plastic jug into the pond to fill it with water. Very gently, pour some of the water into the jar until it's two-thirds full. Pour some of the water in the bowl. Screw on the jug top and keep the rest of the water to take home.

Draw the strainer along the bottom or top of the pond to catch some insects. Dump your catch into the bowl. Make your pick and spoon a few insects into the jar. Don't put in too many or they'll all die from crowding. Quickly put two pieces of cheesecloth over the top of the jar and put a rubber band around it. Dump the insects you don't want back into the pond.

WHIRLIGIG BEETLE

MOSQUITO LARVAE

WATER SCAVENGER BEETLE

At home, keep your aquarium away from direct sunlight and very warm spots. Move it as little as possible so the water won't get cloudy. (Moving the jar will stir up the mud at the bottom.) Don't add food. Your insects will eat the plants—or each other. Add the pond water you brought home as the water in your aquarium evaporates.

P.S. In about a week, return the plants and insects that are left to the pond and get some new ones to watch.

Hint: Don't pick up water insects with your fingers. Some of them bite!

The Amazing Archerfish

The tiny archerfish is a swimming squirt gun. When it sees an insect sitting on a reed or overhanging branch, it gets ready to shoot. Zap! The fish fires drops of water from its mouth to knock a snack off a perch. Although only seven inches long, the archerfish is a real sharpshooter—it can hit a bug five feet away!

A Little Water Music, Please

Water Bells

Line up about eight drinking glasses. It doesn't matter whether they're the same size or different sizes, but they must be made of glass. Put a different amount of water in each one. Tap them with a pencil or spoon to make them ring like bells. You can even play a tune.

P.S. If you change the level of water in a glass, it will produce a different note.

Spray Drums

Take some old metal pots, pot lids, pie plates, cans, and bowls outside. Get a garbage can and lid, a few plastic flowerpots and jugs, and anything else that will thump or rattle when you spray water on it.

Turn the pots, cans, and bowls open-side down on the grass or driveway. Lean the pot lids, pie plates, and garbage-can lid against a wall. Spray everything with plant sprayers or a hose to make drum noises. For the most interesting sounds, use a fine needle spray or a fierce stream. For an outdoor orchestra, add in a few friends with squirt guns.

P.S. Set up an automatic rhythm section by putting lids under a dripping faucet.

Whistling Wineglasses

Besides water and several wineglasses, all you need to make this music is a clean, wet finger. Any glass that has a stem will work as long as it is made of glass.

Put a different amount of water in each glass. Dip your fingertip in water and run it around and around the rim of one of them. Don't press too hard. You may have to go around the rim several times before you hear a weird whistling sound. **Hint:** You have to keep your finger damp to keep the music going.

Now try the other glasses. Each one will make a different sound. Move your finger from glass to glass to make weird music, and for super weird whistle music, do two glasses at once!

Bottle and Jug Tooting Band

For this band, you need at least three kids (but more are better), empty glass bottles (or ceramic jugs), and some water. Put a different amount of water in each bottle. If you have lots of bottles, each kid can toot on two.

To make a bottle toot, blow straight across the open top. Get a rhythm of short and long toots going. Do a knee bend with each toot and see who can keep playing longest without laughing.

Hint: If you can't get your bottle to toot, hold it against your lower lip so that the bottle top is even with the top of your bottom teeth. Blow again.

Simple Salt-Water Distiller

Countries that don't have enough water for people and plants turn salty sea water into fresh water. They distill it to get the salt out. Here's how you can distill water in your kitchen. You need a kettle, a widemouthed jar, a metal soup ladle or spoon that's been chilled in the refrigerator, and two cups of homemade salt water.

Put the salt water in the kettle and start heating it on the stove. (If you're not allowed to use the stove by yourself, ask someone older to help.) Get your jar and cold soup ladle ready. Soon after the water starts boiling, clouds of steam will come out of the kettle's spout. Hold the soup ladle to catch the steam. The jar should be right underneath the ladle. Little drops of water will fall from the soup ladle into the jar. Do this until all the water in the kettle has boiled away.

Taste the water in the jar. Surprise! When the kettle has cooled, run your finger around the inside bottom of it and you'll find out what happened to salt. (Don't forget to rinse out the kettle when you clean up.)

HOW TO MAKE HOMEMADE
SALT WATER:

Just add salt to tap water and stir until the salt dissolves. Keep adding and stirring until the water tastes pretty salty.

Potato Pollution-Detector

A potato can tell you if water is polluted. Make a few potato pollution-detectors so you can test several kinds of water at the same time. Try samples of pond water, lake water, stream water, water from a street puddle, tap water, bottled water, rain water, even dew. Use a clean, dry container to collect each sample.

For each detector, tape a piece of paper to the side of a clean, dry jar with a screw-on lid. Then peel and boil some small potatoes. Cut them in half and put each half in a jar. Pour a different sample of water into each jar. The water should come only halfway up the potato. Make sure you label each jar before you pour the next sample. Screw on the lids and put the jars in a warm, dark place.

In a few days, look at the potato in each jar. If you see fuzzy stuff growing on it, the water sample in that jar is polluted. The more fuzzy stuff there is, the more polluted the water is.

P.S. There shouldn't be any fuzzy stuff on the potato in the tap water or the bottled water!

CATCHING DEW:

Dig a small, shallow pit in the ground. Spread out a small sheet of plastic (a garbage bag will do) and poke its center into the pit. Put stones on the corners to keep it in place. Leave it overnight. In the morning, pick the plastic sheet up carefully by the corners and pour the dew it's collected into a jar.

Water-Drop Magnifier

To make a drop of water into a magnifying glass, follow these steps:

1. Cut a circle about 1½ inches (4 centimeters) across in the center of a square piece of cardboard that's 6 inches (15 centimeters) on each side.

2. Fold two sides of the cardboard under to make legs about 1 inch (2.5 centimeters) high. Then fold each leg in half. Tape the legs so they look like this:

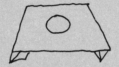

3. Cut a piece of clear plastic food wrap and place it over the hole. Keep smoothing the plastic as you tape each corner so it ends up without wrinkles.

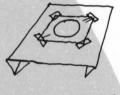

4. Dip a toothpick into water. Gently shake a drop of water from it onto the plastic. Do this two more times to make a medium-sized drop on the plastic. (Add more drops from the toothpick to make the drop on the plastic bigger. Touch the drop with a bit of paper towel to make it smaller.)

Use your magnifier near a sunny window or a bright light. Put a dead bug, a postage stamp, a page with tiny print, salt crystals, or whatever else you want to look at on a piece of white paper. Slide the paper under the cardboard and look at your object through the drop of water. Experiment with different sizes of water drops. Which size magnifies best?

Spatter Platter

On a rainy day, let the rain make an instant painting for you. Dribble a few drops and blobs of food coloring, poster paint, or ink on a paper plate (a regular white paper plate, not a plastic-coated one). Don't mix the drops or spread them around. Put the plate outside in the rain (or even hold it out the window). It may take only half a minute for the rain to spatter the drops on the paper plate into a painting, so watch the plate carefully. When you like the pattern the rain has made, bring the plate inside to dry.

Liquid Sculpture

Oil and water don't mix. That's why this kind of sculpture works. You'll need one jar with a watertight screw-on lid. Fill the jar up halfway with water. Add drops of food coloring to color the water. (Or use ink.) Then fill the jar to the top with mineral oil or vegetable oil. Pour gently. Screw the lid on very tight, hold the jar sideways, and then roll or rock the jar back and forth a few times to get your sculpture moving.

Water Magic

Water is naturally tricky. With only a few props and an audience, you can be a water magician right away.

The Upside-Down Water Glass Trick

With something sharp and pointed (like a compass point), carefully poke a lot of small holes in a square piece of stiff cardboard about 4½ inches (11 centimeters) on each side. Fill a glass with water until it starts to overflow. Show your audience the cardboard and let them see the holes. Then put the cardboard across the top of the glass. It's okay if some of the water squishes out. Keep one hand pressed flat on the cardboard as you turn the glass over with your other hand. Say a few magic words, like abracadabra or alla-kazam, and tell your audience that your magic will keep the water from coming out the holes. Take your hand away from the card-board with a flourish—the water won't come out!

The Floating-and-Sinking Pin Trick

Put out on a table a bunch of straight pins, some small paper clips, and a glass that's filled to the brim with water. Ask your audience to try floating the pins and paper clips on the water. (They won't be able to unless they know the secret of this trick.)

Tell the audience you can float pins and paper clips with your magic fork and then get them to sink without ever touching them. Scoop a pin onto a table fork. Gently lay the fork on the edge of the glass. Say some magic words as you carefully tilt the fork into the water until the pin is floating. Float a few more pins and a paper clip or two. Then say some magic words as you touch the water's surface lightly with a tiny piece of soap. Everything will sink. You'll have to rinse the glass thoroughly and refill it if you want to do the trick again.

P.S. If you want to float heavier things (like bigger paper clips or safety pins), stir a tablespoon of salt in the water.

The Bent Water Trick

You need these props: a blown-up balloon, a piece of *wool* cloth (or a wool sock, scarf, or coat), and a water faucet.

Turn on the faucet so that a *very thin* stream of water comes out. Tell your audience that your magic balloon can bend the stream of water. Say a few magic words as you rub the balloon hard and fast against the piece of wool. Then hold the balloon a few inches from the stream of water. The water will bend out towards the balloon!

HINT:

Don't forget to practice these tricks by yourself before you perform them for an audience!

Underwater Binoculars

Recycle old milk cartons into underwater binoculars. You can use them to see stuff underwater clearly while you're leaning over the side of a pier or boat or just standing in shallow water. You will need:

- 2 clean 1-quart (1-liter) milk cartons (for giant binocs, use ½-gallon or 2-liter cartons)
- a jar lid about 2¼ inches (6 centimeters) across
- clear plastic food wrap
- 2 big rubber bands
- tape, scissors, and a pencil
- a very sharp, small knife
- an emery board or sandpaper

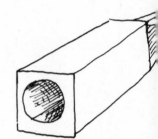

Trace a circle on the bottom of each carton, using the jar lid as a guide. Then cut out the circles very slowly and carefully with the knife. Take your time! Smooth the edges of each hole by rubbing them with the emery board.

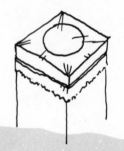

Hold one carton between your knees and stretch a layer of plastic wrap over the bottom to make a lens. Put a rubber band around the wrap so it stays smooth. Trim off the extra wrap, leaving about ½ inch or 2 centimeters below the rubber band.

Tape down the edge of the plastic wrap with little bits of tape this way: Tape one side and then the opposite side. Keep taping alternate sides all the way around so that the plastic stays smooth over the hole. The tape shouldn't touch the rubber band. Then seal the lens by running a long strip of tape all around the edge of the wrap. Put the lens on the other carton the same way. Carefully take off the rubber bands.

Stand the cartons side by side on a table, lens end down. Open the spouts so you can look down at the lenses. Then slide the rubber bands over both cartons to hold them together. Your binocs should look like this: ⟶

To use the binoculars, stick them just below the water.

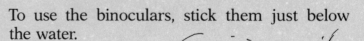

WINDPLAY

Paper Plate Flying Saucer

This simple flying saucer is a snap to make and flies like crazy on a breezy day. Just staple two 9-inch paper plates together back to back. (Regular paper plates are okay, but plastic-coated ones are sturdier and fly farther.) If the wind is right, the saucer will dip, swoop, float, and even make S curves. Throw it into the wind and it'll come back to you!

PUT IN EIGHT STAPLES LIKE THIS:

FLING BACKHAND TO GIVE THE SAUCER A GOOD SPIN

YOU AND A FRIEND CAN TOSS IT BACK AND FORTH — OR TRY TO!

64

Sidewalk Sail Car

When leaves are blowing along the ground, you've got a perfect day for racing a sail car on the sidewalk. To make one, you will need:

- a paper-towel tube cut in half
- a piece of heavy cardboard
- an index card (or any stiff card), 4 inches by 6 inches or 10 centimeters by 15 centimeters
- 2 plastic straws
- 3 skinny sticks or pieces of wire, longer than the straws
- a pencil
- a big rubber band
- a compass (the kind you use to draw circles)
- scissors

1. Stretch the rubber band lengthwise around the middle of the tube. Make a set of holes at each end of the tube by poking the compass point through both sides just above the rubber band. Remove the rubber band and enlarge the holes with a pencil.

2. Slide a straw through each pair of holes. Slide a stick through each straw to make an axle.

3. Use the compass to draw 4 wheels 2½ inches (6 centimeters) across on the piece of heavy cardboard. (The distance between the compass point and the pencil should be 1¼ inches or 3 centimeters.) Cut the wheels out. Push them on the axles so they nearly touch the straws.

4. Use the compass point to poke holes for the mast in the center top and bottom of the tube. Push the third stick into the holes. Cut slits in the index-card sail and slide it on the mast.

Now just set your sail car on a sidewalk and watch wind power make it go!

Hints: If the wind is blowing your car over, clip paper clips on the front and back of the tube for extra weight. Try setting the sail at different angles if your car won't go straight.

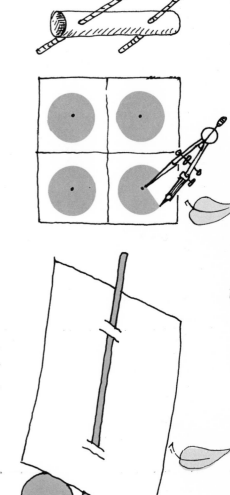

NO FANNING ALLOWED IN RACES!

Wind Streamer

Is the wind steady enough for good kite flying? Which direction should you point your sail car or styrofoam trimaran (pages 65 and 51) for top speed? Set up a wind streamer to find out. All you need are a nail with a large head that's at least 1½ inches (4 centimeters) long, a clothespin with a spring, a strip of brightly colored cloth about a foot (30 centimeters) long, a long stick (like a mop handle), and a hammer.

Slide the nail through the spring in the clothespin. Hammer it only partway into one end of the stick so the clothespin can spin around on it.

Shove the stick into the ground in an open spot, away from buildings and trees. Clip one end of the cloth to the clothespin and your streamer is all set.

How to read your wind streamer:
- When it doesn't move, that's easy—there's no wind!
- If it sticks out straight and stays that way, there's a good steady wind that will keep a kite flying.
- If it flops up and down, the wind is gusty, and you'll have trouble keeping a kite up.
- To catch the most wind, aim your sail car or trimaran in the direction that the streamer is pointing.

Whirling Wind Vane

A quick look at a wind vane will tell you which direction—north, south, east, or west—the wind is coming from. The vane's arrow will always be pointing in that direction.

Here's what you need to make a wind vane:

- the top cap of a ball-point pen
- a broomstick or mop handle with one flat end
- 2 popsicle sticks (or tongue depressors)
- a piece of stiff wire about 8 inches long
- a clean milk carton
- scissors
- a pencil
- a felt marking pen (one with permanent ink)
- paper clips
- heavy tape
- a hammer and tacks
- a ruler

Here's what you do:

1. Cut out two arrows from the sides of the milk carton. Use your ruler to help you make them this size and shape:

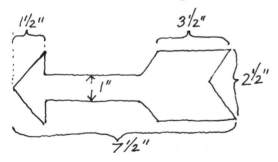

2. Tape the arrows together with the top cap of a ball-point pen between them, like this:

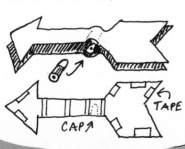

3. Pick an open spot in your yard. Shove the broomstick in the ground with the flat end up. Pound it down with a hammer to make it steady.

4. Cross the two popsicle sticks and label them N, E, S, and W (for north, east, south, and west) with the marking pen. They should look like this:

5. Tack the popsicle sticks together on top of the broomstick. Don't pound them in too hard. Twist them until they point in the right directions. (Ask somebody where north is if you're not sure, or use a compass to find it.)

6. Tape the wire to the broomstick so that it sticks up above the popsicle sticks. Put the arrow on the wire. (Make sure you fit the wire into the cap.) If the arrow dips to the front or back, put paper clips on the back or front to balance it.

When you want to know what direction the wind is coming from, just check to see which popsicle stick is pointing in the same direction as the arrow.

Super Space Shuttle

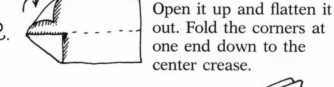

1. Fold an 8½- by 11-inch sheet of paper in half like this.

2. Open it up and flatten it out. Fold the corners at one end down to the center crease.

3.  Fold the folded corners over to the center crease.

4. Fold up the sides along the center crease.

5.

Don't make this bottom part too big, or you won't have much of a wingspan.

Now fold most of each side down to make wings.

6.  Staple or tape the nose to keep it together. Add two small paper clips to the front of the wings.

7.

Tape the back of the body to keep it together.

8. Attach a one-inch section of paper-towel or toilet-paper tube to the back with two small paper clips, one on either side of the center.

Launch gently in a light breeze!

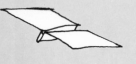
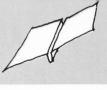

Simple Paper Glider

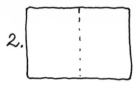
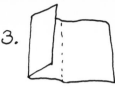

1.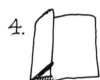

Fold a sheet of paper in half.

2.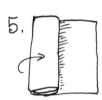

Open it up and flatten it out.

3.

Fold one side to the center crease.

4.

Fold the folded part to the center crease.

5.

Flip the folded part over the crease.

6.

Fold the whole thing in half crosswise.

7.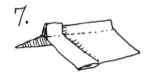

Fold back most of each side and crease to make wings.

8.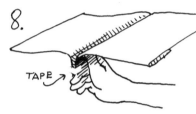

TAPE →

Hold the glider by the body. Tape the nose together.

Let it glide in the wind!

Paper Airplane Races

Get some friends together and test your paper airplanes in these races.

Race #1   Rocket Launch
Stand behind a line. Launch your paper airplanes at the word "Go." When they land, see whose airplane went the farthest. Do this at least five times. The kid whose airplane flies the farthest in the most rounds is the winner.

Race #2   Space Race (A Cross-Country Event)
For this race, you need a big, open field. All the kids line up with their paper airplanes at one end. At the word "Go," everybody launches his or her paper airplane and runs after it. When airplanes land, they are launched again, but they have to come to a complete stop first. (No fair running with a plane, either!) The kid whose airplane gets to the other end of the field first is the winner.

A Windy Day Recipe

Add a bunch of bubbles to the next good breeze. For sure-fire, long-lasting, great big bubbles, use this formula:

  2 cups clean warm water
  6 tablespoons glycerine (Buy this at a drugstore.)
  6 tablespoons liquid dishwashing detergent
  a dash of sugar

Mix the ingredients in a clean bowl. Beat the mixture with an eggbeater or a wire whisk.

To make bubble blowers:

Bend one end of a wire into a loop.

Or cut the end of a straw like this:

Or punch a hole in the bottom of a paper cup.

Or for a super minibubble blower, tape seven straws together like this:

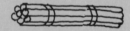

Outside, dip your blower into the bubble mix and . . .

Let the wind blow your bubbles for you.
Watch the bubbles float on a gusty wind.
Play float and catch by yourself or with a friend.
Chase bubbles until the wind blows them down.

Windy Day Costumes

On a day when the wind is strong and steady, put on one of these costumes and just start running into the wind. It won't be hard to imagine that you're a bird or a bat or a butterfly or Superman or anything else that flies. (But don't forget to watch where you're going!)

Sheet Cape

Cut a big piece from an old sheet and decorate it with felt markers. Hold it over your shoulders as you run.

Bat Wings

Cut a bat wing shape from a black trash bag made of heavy plastic. Make it as long as the distance from one hand to the other when your arms are stretched out to the sides. Cut a narrow piece of cardboard the same length. Staple or tape the top edge of your wings to one side of the cardboard strip. Staple 4 loops of elastic big enough to fit around your hands and arms to the other side of the cardboard. Slide your arms and hands in the loops and take off!

Streamers

Staple or tape long pieces of crepe paper or long strips of colored cloth to an old cloth belt or a long, narrow strip cut from an old sheet. Stretch out your arms and hold the ends of the belt or strip of sheet in your hands as you run.

Make a Mini Box Kite

This kite isn't very big, but you can fly it in places where a big kite couldn't get off the ground—on a sidewalk or between buildings. To make it, you'll need:

- a piece of thin cardboard at least 8 inches by 9¼ inches (half a file folder works well)
- a spool of extra strong thread, like carpet thread
- a ruler
- a sharp knife
- a pencil
- tape
- scissors

Draw this pattern on your piece of thin cardboard. Cut it out. Use a sharp knife to cut out the three windows. Be careful! (If you're not allowed to use knives, ask someone older for help.) Then fold the cardboard in three places, just under the windows. Run the edge of your ruler back and forth over each fold to make a sharp crease.

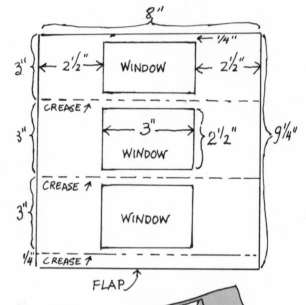

Now make your three-cornered box kite by folding the cardboard into this shape: —————▶
Tape the flap.

Loop the thread through the kite and tie it so the thread looks like this: —————

Put the pencil through the thread spool so you can hold on to it and let the thread unwind easily.

If you can't wait for the next windy day, test-fly your kite in front of a big fan.

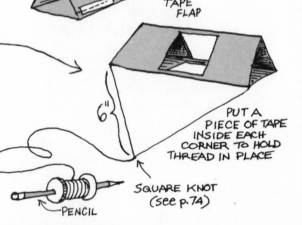

Hints on Kite-Flying

1. For good kite-flying, a steady wind is more important than a strong wind.
2. To launch a kite, hold the kite string in one hand and the spool in the other and run—not too fast—into the wind. Be sure to watch where you're going! If it's really windy, you won't have to run.
3. Let the kite up a little at a time.
4. Don't fly a kite near wires, traffic, or trees, and never fly one in stormy weather.
5. If you're flying a big kite, fly it in a big open field or parking lot.

Trash-Bag Sled Kite

This flying sled really soars! Besides a heavy plastic trash bag, at least 22 inches by 24 inches, the only supplies you need are: cloth tape, a ball of strong string (at least 20-pound test weight), and 3 sticks 24 inches long. (Use sticks of thin bamboo or ¼ inch balsa or ⅛ inch dowels.) You'll need these tools: a yardstick, scissors, a hole puncher, and felt marking pens.

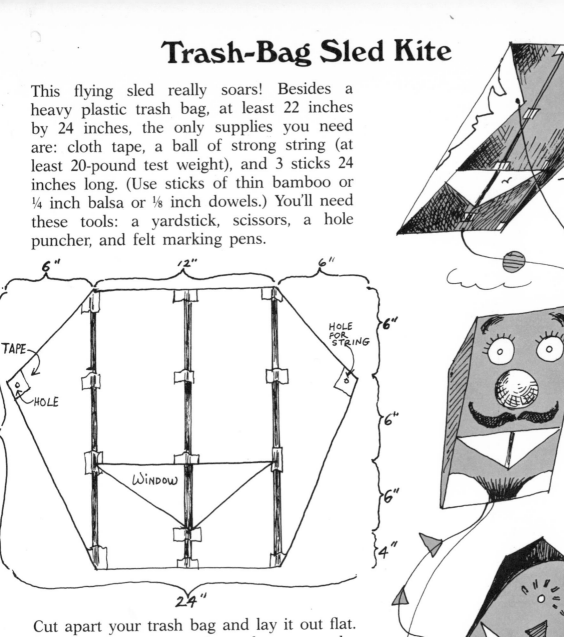

Cut apart your trash bag and lay it out flat. Draw the pattern on it, and cut out the kite shape and the window. Then tape on the sticks. At the top, bottom, and window edges of the kite, fold the tape over the edges. Fold tape over each side corner and punch a hole in the center of the tape.

Tie one end of a 4-foot piece of string to one side of the kite and the other end to the other side. Tie your ball of string to the center of that string. (Use square knots! See page 74.)

Use felt marking pens to decorate your kite any way you want. You don't need a tail on your kite to make it fly. But if you think a tail would look nice, tape one to the bottom of the center stick. Just use a piece of string with bows taped on it or a long piece of brightly colored ribbon.

How to Tie a Square Knot

Use this strong knot when you're making a kite. It won't come undone.

1. Hold one end of string in each hand.

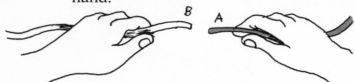

2. Cross the end in your right hand (A) over the end in your left hand (B). Pull end A under end B, then pull end A up. (Think of this step as "right over left and under.")

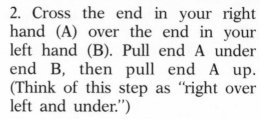

3. Cross end A over end B again. Pull end A under end B again, then up. (Think of this step as "left over right and under.")

4. Pull the two ends away from each other to tighten the knot.

Very Windy Facts

Did you know . . .
- that the highest wind ever measured was 231 miles (372 kilometers) per hour on Mt. Washington in New Hampshire on April 12, 1934?
- that the windiest place in the world day in and day out is the Commonwealth Bay on the George V coast of Antarctica, where winds often reach 200 miles (322 kilometers) per hour?
- that the winds rotating inside a tornado may hit 600 miles (almost 1,000 kilometers) per hour?

Windy Disasters in the U.S.: Tornado Power

- On March 18, 1925, a tornado in the Midwest that traveled 219 miles through six states killed 689 people and totally destroyed 35 towns.
- A series of 100 tornadoes hit 11 states on April 3 and 4, 1974, killing 324 people and causing $400,000,000 worth of damage. Half of Xenia, Ohio, was destroyed in five minutes. In Indiana, the wind lifted a factory warehouse right off the ground and put it down a mile away.

The Beaufort Wind Scale

Be a wind expert. Just look at what's happening outside, and you can start using the Beaufort scale. (It's pronounced BO-fort.) This scale is a way of telling how strong the wind is by watching how the wind blows things. It was invented by a British admiral, Sir Francis Beaufort, in 1805. It works so well that people (and weather bureaus) still use it today.

WHAT HAPPENS	WIND DESCRIPTION	WIND SPEED MILES PER HOUR	BEAUFORT FORCE NUMBER
SMOKE RISES STRAIGHT UP.	CALM	LESS THAN 1	0
SMOKE DRIFTS SLOWLY.	LIGHT AIR	1-3	1
LEAVES RUSTLE, WIND CAN BE FELT ON FACE.	SLIGHT BREEZE	4-7	2
LEAVES AND TWIGS MOVE, SMALL FLAGS WAVE.	GENTLE BREEZE	8-12	3
DUST AND PAPER BLOW AROUND, SMALL BRANCHES MOVE.	MODERATE BREEZE	13-18	4
SMALL TREES SWAY.	FRESH BREEZE	19-24	5
BRANCHES ON BIG TREES SWAY, UMBRELLAS ARE HARD TO HANDLE.	STRONG BREEZE	25-31	6
BIG TREES SWAY, WALKING AGAINST WIND IS DIFFICULT.	HIGH WINDS	32-38	7
TWIGS BREAK OFF TREES, WALKING AGAINST THE WIND IS VERY DIFFICULT.	FRESH GALE	39-46	8
BRANCHES BREAK OFF TREES, ANTENNAS BLOW DOWN.	STRONG GALE	47-54	9
TREES ARE UPROOTED.	WHOLE GALE	55-63	10
BUILDINGS ARE DAMAGED.	STORM	64-74	11
EXTREME DAMAGE TO BUILDINGS, COUNTRYSIDE DEVASTATED.	HURRICANE	ABOVE 74	12

Wind Chimes

Hang a wind chime in front of an open window or from the branch of a tree, and you'll hear tinkly sounds every time a breeze blows through it.

Make this wind chime from a plastic food cup (about 4 inches or 10 centimeters across), string, tape, and lots of little hard plastic lids or empty pill containers.

Poke four holes in the bottom of the cup. Poke as many holes around the top edge as the number of plastic bits you have. Make all the holes with a pin first, and then enlarge them with a pencil. Thread a piece of string at least 24 inches (61 centimeters) long through the four holes in the bottom of the cup, the way the picture shows. Tie the ends together.

Cut pieces of string about 10 inches (25 centimeters) long—as many pieces as you have plastic bits. Tape one end of each string to the bottom of a pill container or lid. To hang each plastic bit, push the other end of the string through a hole in the edge of the cup. Tie a knot in it. **Hint:** Make sure you don't hang all the heaviest plastic bits on one side.

Adjust the string in the bottom of the cup so the chime hangs straight.

Variations

Shell Wind Chime: Tape strings of sea shells to the inside rim of a small plastic or clay flowerpot. Tie a big knot in a heavy piece of string. Pull the string through the hole in the bottom of the flowerpot so the knot catches on the inside.

Bamboo Wind Chime: Tape pieces of string to short bamboo tubes. Tie each piece of string around a bamboo stick. Thread a long piece of string through the bamboo stick and tie the ends together.

Pint-Sized Parachutes

On a windy day, toss a parachute in the air and let the wind do the rest. You can make miniature parachutes out of plastic bags, tissue paper, or paper napkins. You'll also need strong thread, tape, two paper clips, and a weight, such as a cork, a tiny block of wood, or a film can with two coins in it. Here's how to make your parachute:

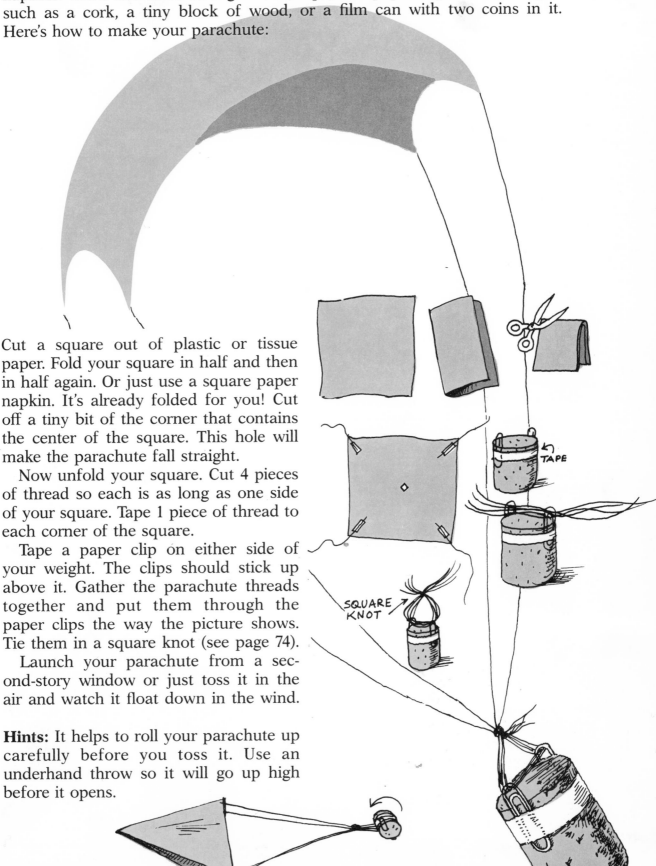

Cut a square out of plastic or tissue paper. Fold your square in half and then in half again. Or just use a square paper napkin. It's already folded for you! Cut off a tiny bit of the corner that contains the center of the square. This hole will make the parachute fall straight.

Now unfold your square. Cut 4 pieces of thread so each is as long as one side of your square. Tape 1 piece of thread to each corner of the square.

Tape a paper clip on either side of your weight. The clips should stick up above it. Gather the parachute threads together and put them through the paper clips the way the picture shows. Tie them in a square knot (see page 74).

Launch your parachute from a second-story window or just toss it in the air and watch it float down in the wind.

Hints: It helps to roll your parachute up carefully before you toss it. Use an underhand throw so it will go up high before it opens.

TAPE

SQUARE KNOT

Pinwheel Mobile

This lightweight sculpture turns and twirls in the lightest breeze. You'll need lots of pinwheels, so get busy. To make a pinwheel, you need:

- a balsa stick or small cardboard tube (the kind that comes on wire clothes hangers)
- a piece of paper
- a pencil
- scissors
- a ruler
- a straight pin
- a tiny piece of thin cardboard
- (You'll also need strong thread, like carpet thread, to make the mobile after you've finished the pinwheels.)

First cut out a paper square that's 4 inches (10 centimeters) on each side. Draw straight lines from corner to opposite corner (use the ruler). Where the lines cross is the center of the square. Poke a hole there with the pin. Cut down each line from the corner, stopping ½ inch (1.5 centimeters) before the center hole.

Poke holes in the corners the way the picture shows.

Curl each corner toward the center and slip its hole on the point of the pin. Do the holes in order—1, 2, 3, then 4. When they're all on, push the pin through the center hole.

To complete the pinwheel, stick the pin into the tiny piece of cardboard and then into the end of the balsa stick. (If you use a cardboard tube, then just stick the pin into the *side* of the end of the tube.)

Make as many pinwheels as you want, and then make the mobile. Use the thread to hang each balsa stick from another one. Balance each stick by sliding the thread it's hanging from back and forth until the stick is horizontal. Hang the mobile near your window to catch the breeze.

SNOWPLAY

Snowbutton, Snowbutton

To play this game, you need four or more friends, some snow, and a brightly colored button. Make three plain snowballs and one snowball with the button hidden inside it. Then choose someone to be *It*. Everyone else stands in a circle around *It* and passes the snowballs quickly around the circle. When *It* says "Stop," he or she guesses which person has the snowball with the button inside. Kids holding snowballs break them open to see which one has the button. If *It*'s guess is correct, the one who has the button is *It* next. If *It* is wrong, he or she is *It* again.

Snow Puppets

Chill some popsicle sticks or pencils in the freezer. Make some small, hard-packed snowballs. Carefully stick one popsicle stick into each snowball and pack the snow around the spot where you stuck it in. Make a miniature snowperson's face on the snowball with small things like tiny buttons, dried kidney beans, raisins, thumbtacks, orange lentils, or anything else you can think of. Use your imagination! Tape a piece of fabric or tie a ribbon around the popsicle stick. Build a snow wall to crouch behind while you put on a snow puppet play.

Snow Job

When it's cold and snowy, there's nothing people like better than something hot to drink. Have fun and make money by running a hot drink stand. Here's what you need to set it up:

> paper or styrofoam cups intended for hot drinks
> 2 or 3 thermos bottles containing hot drinks
> a trash can and trash bags
> two cardboard cartons and a wide board to use as a stand
> signs telling what the drinks are and what they cost
> a box of change (at least two dollars' worth)

Now for some hot drink ideas. Hot chocolate looks fancy if you top each cup with a marshmallow. Hot cranberry juice tastes extra delicious when you add lemon slices. Hot apple juice or cider is good plain, but to add a spicy taste, put in a few cloves while you're heating it. Heat juice or cider in a pan over medium heat. Don't let it boil. To make the hot chocolate, follow the directions on a package of hot cocoa mix. (Get help if you're not allowed to use the stove by yourself.)

Add up how much the cups, hot drink ingredients, and trash bags cost. Then figure out how many drinks you've made. One quart of juice or hot chocolate usually equals four to six drinks, depending on the size of your cups. Divide how much everything costs by how many drinks you have to sell. Add 5¢ to the answer. That's about how much to charge for each drink.

Keep the trash can next to your stand so people have a place to throw their used cups.

P.S. If you raid your parents' kitchen for supplies, don't forget to pay for them!

Bird-Feeder Snowperson

Make a hard, solid snowball and roll it around in the snow to make it bigger. Pack the snow around it until the ball gets so heavy that just rolling it packs on snow. When the ball is about 2½ feet (76 centimeters) high, roll it to a sunny spot near a tree or bush. Make two smaller balls of snow for the middle and the head, and then stack them on the big ball. If they're too heavy for you to lift by yourself, get a few friends to help.

This snowperson's for the birds, so give it a pine cone stuffed with peanut butter for a nose, dates for eyes, a line of raisins for a mouth, and chopped apples for buttons. String cranberries on strong thread to make a belt. Top off your snowperson with an old straw beach hat that nobody wants and sprinkle bird seed and sunflower seeds on the brim. Make arms from thick twigs so there's somewhere for the birds to perch while eating. Nearby put a pail of water filled close to the top so there's something for them to drink.

P.S. Check the water every morning. If it's frozen, break the layer of ice so the birds will be able to get water.

Be a Snow Snoop

Anything that walks on snow leaves tracks. The morning after a snowfall, find out what's been going on in your neighborhood. A good snow snoop can figure out what left tracks, where it went, and what it did on the way.

Here are some tracks to look for:

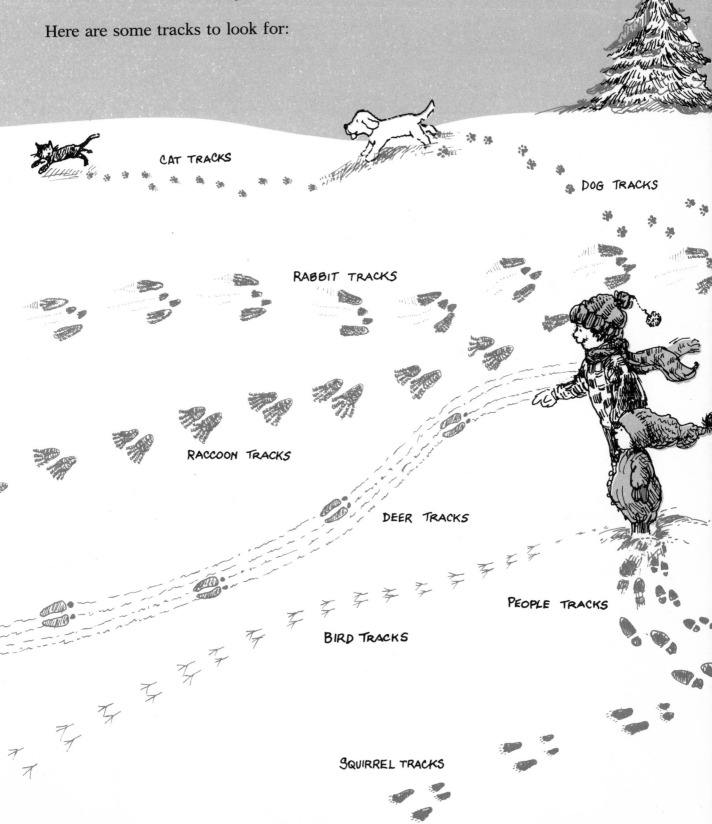

CAT TRACKS

DOG TRACKS

RABBIT TRACKS

RACCOON TRACKS

DEER TRACKS

PEOPLE TRACKS

BIRD TRACKS

SQUIRREL TRACKS

Mad Snow Facts

MAD FACT #1

The world record for the deepest snowfall within 24 hours is 6 feet 4 inches (1.9 meters) at Silver Lake, Colorado, on April 14 and 15, 1921.

MAD FACT #2

And the world record for a single snowfall is 14 feet 7½ inches (4.5 meters) after a five-day snowstorm in Thompson's Pass, Alaska, from December 26 to December 31, 1955.

Make a Snow Gauge

During the next snowstorm, use a snow gauge to check out how much snow falls in your yard. You'll need a 2- or 3-pound coffee can, a felt marking pen (one with permanent ink in it), and a ruler.

Make a line inside the coffee can for each inch (or centimeter) and label the lines 1, 2, 3, and so on, from the bottom up. When it starts to snow, put the can out on the ground in an open spot, away from trees, buildings, and fences. Check to see how many inches (or centimeters) of snow have fallen when the snowstorm is over or after each 24-hour period.

How Deep Is the Drift?

Use a yardstick (or meterstick) as a snowdrift measurer. Push it down in the snow until the end touches the ground. (Make sure you put the end that starts with 1 inch or 1 centimeter in the snow!) See how deep the snow is next to trees, up against buildings, next to fences, on driveways or streets, and in different spots in yards. Find the deepest drift. Keep a neighborhood record of how deep the deepest drifts are and where they are. Do you think the deepest drifts will be in shady, sunny, or windy spots?

Taking Snow Temperatures

Make your snowdrift measurer into a snow temperature-taker and find out how cold the snow is. Tie or tape an old outdoor thermometer to the end of your yardstick or meterstick (see the picture). Be sure you don't put the tape over the bulb. Gently push your temperature-taker into a snowdrift, thermometer end first. It will take a little time for the thermometer to adjust to the snow's temperature, so leave it there for a few minutes. Try deep snow and shallow snow, snow in shady spots, and snow in sunny spots.

Is snow always colder than the air? Check the air temperature by turning the yardstick upside down so the thermometer is sticking up in the air. Don't forget to wait for a few minutes before you read it.

Snowprints

What a big patch of new snow needs for decoration is some snowprints. Make a bunch by yourself or with friends. All you have to do is lie down on your back in the snow and move your arms and legs back and forth. Presto! There's a snowprint! Try these snowprints for starters.

TREE

ANGEL

ROCKET

BUTTERFLY

P.S. DON'T STOP NOW.
MAKE UP SOME MORE.

Fox and Geese

Playing this game is a good way to keep warm on a cold day because it keeps you moving. You need five (or more) players and a snowy area with no footprints. First walk around to make a big circle of footprints in the snow. Tramp two paths across the circle. (Stay only on the paths.) Where the paths cross in the center, stamp down a small area of snow to make a "safe zone." Choose one person to be the "fox." Everyone else is a "goose."

Now you're ready to start playing. The fox chases the geese, trying to tag one of them. Everyone must run only on the paths. As soon as the fox tags a goose, that goose becomes the new fox. But there's a way to catch your breath without getting caught. A goose standing in the safe zone can't be tagged.

Snow Scientist

You can prove that snowflakes are just frozen water and that snow is just snowflakes with air between them by doing this experiment.

You will need:

- 2 jars or glasses that are the same size
- a pen or pencil
- masking tape
- a ruler
- some snow

Put a piece of tape on each jar so you can label it. Go outside and fill one jar with fluffy snow, but don't pack it down. With the pen, mark that jar "Fluffy Snow." Pack snow into the second jar. Make sure you pack it down hard. Mark it "Packed Snow." Bring the jars inside and let the snow melt. **Hint:** To make the snow melt faster put the jars in a pan of hot water.

How many inches of water do you get in each jar? Do you get more water from the packed snow or the fluffy snow? Is there more air in the packed snow or the fluffy snow? Why? If you're not sure why, turn the page upside down and read the explanation below.

Answer: There's more water and less air in the jar of packed snow because when you packed the snow, you squished out some air. So you had room for more snowflakes in the jar. That's why you got more water.

Eskimo Snow Goggles

Be the first kid on your block to make Eskimo snow goggles. The snow is extra bright when sun shines on it because snow reflects light. Your Eskimo snow goggles will cut the glare. To make them, you will need heavy cardboard (a shirt cardboard is good), a piece of string about 3 feet or 1 meter long, sharp-pointed scissors, a pencil, and a ruler.

Cut out a piece of cardboard 6 inches (15 centimeters) long and 2 inches (5 centimeters) high. Hold it up to your face and have a friend or parent carefully mark on it where your eyes are. Using a ruler and a pencil, draw two slits about 1½ inches (4 centimeters) long and about ⅛ inch (.3 centimeters) high for your eyes. Stick the point of one scissors blade into the end of an eye slit, and cut the slit out. Cut out the other eye slit the same way. Check the position of the slits by holding the cardboard up to your eyes. Can you see? Now make a notch for your nose and poke two holes on each side of the goggles. Loop one end of the string through the holes on one side and tie it. Loop the other end through the holes on the other side. Pull that string end tight when you put your goggles on and then tie it.

While you're wearing your snow goggles, impress your friends by saying Eskimo words for the kinds of snow you see:

aniuq (AN-yook) means snow on the ground
nepcalluk (NEP-cha-luk) means wet, sticky snow
meciqaq (me-CHEE-kak) means water-soaked snow
qaninerraq (ka-NEE-ner-rak) means freshly fallen soft snow

Snow Brick & Building Company

Get your snow building company going by making snow bricks. You can use them to build anything from a snow wall to a complete snow fort. A metal bread or meat-loaf pan makes the best brick mold. Pack snow into the mold, turn it upside down, tap the bottom of the mold lightly, and you have a snow brick. If the snow is too dry to pack well, sprinkle water very lightly on some snow before packing it in the mold.

Whatever you're building, build each wall layer by layer. Place the bricks side by side (long sides together) so the wall will be good and thick. Lightly pack snow in the gaps between the bricks.

Dog Sled Express

It takes a long time to haul a big supply of snowballs or snow bricks to a snow fort . . . unless you have a dog sled. If you have a good-natured dog that likes to play in the snow, it might not mind being a sled dog. Get two pieces of light rope and a sled. Tie one rope to one side of your dog's collar and the second to the other side. Tie the other ends of the ropes to the front corners of your sled. Attach a leash to the dog's collar and practice guiding your dog before you load the sled.

And remember: Your dog may get tired of being a sled dog pretty quickly, so don't keep it tied up for long.

Quick Mitts

All you need for a terrific snowball-making contest is some kids, snow that's not too dry or powdery, and a watch or timer. Have one person tell everybody when to start and when to stop. Try these ideas and make up some of your own. Who can make—

the biggest snowball in one minute?
the most snowballs in three minutes?
the tallest snowball tower in five minutes?

Snowball Sharpshooting

You need one *old* sheet or blanket, a clothesline, clothespins, scissors, and all the snowballs you just made. Hang the clothesline up outdoors. Cut three or four holes, about 8 to 12 inches (20 to 30 centimeters) across, in the sheet. Fasten the sheet to the clothesline with lots of clothespins. Stand about 10 feet or 3 meters from the sheet and try to throw the snowballs through the holes. When you're a real sharpshooter, stand farther away. Each snowball that goes through a hole is worth one point. If you're playing by yourself, see how many snowballs it takes you to make five points. If you're playing with a partner, the first person to make five points wins.

Tug-of-Snow-War

Tug-of-war is the most fun in powdery snow. You need a big mound of snow, a good long rope, and at least four kids. Put the rope across the snow mound. You know the rest. Half the kids grab the rope on one side of the mound and the other half grab it on the other side. Everybody pulls. Guess what'll happen to the kids on the losing team!

Silly Snow Sliders

Are you one of those kids with downhill-speed fever? There's more than one way to get to the bottom of a snowy hill. Try these homemade sliders on a nice round hill covered with packed-down snow.

- Beach floats and inner tubes make super sleds. For a race, rub the bottoms with paste wax. Watch out for rocks!
- Use a large piece of corrugated cardboard for an instant bobsled or toboggan. Sit near the front end, curl it up, and hold it tight. Have three kids sit behind you and hold on to you—if they can—as you head downhill.
- If you're not too big, squeeze into a large plastic dishpan for a quick downhill trip. The trick is to get down the slope without falling out of the pan.

ICICLES

MINIATURE ICE CUBES

MILK CARTON TOWER

FUNNEL MOLD

ICE CUBE WALLS

ICE CREAM CARTON TOWER

SANDWICH BOX DRAWBRIDGE

Ice Cube Castle

Create your own backyard fairyland by making a castle from molded ice. The most important thing you need is weather that's below freezing (under 32° F or 0° C). Your castle will last as long as the freezing weather does.

Find some interestingly shaped plastic, metal, or watertight cardboard containers to use as molds. Try fancy cooking molds, styrofoam egg cartons, tiny ice cube trays, plastic funnels plugged with clay or gum, and milk cartons. **Hints:** Be sure the molds are bigger at the top than the bottom and shaped so that you'll be able to get the molded ice out. Don't use glass molds—they may crack when the water freezes.

Take your molds outside and fill them with water. Leave them outside overnight to freeze solid.

To unmold the ice shapes, dip each mold into a bucket of warm water for a few seconds. Then turn it upside down so the ice slides out. **Hints:** Don't touch a cold metal mold with your bare hands—they might freeze to the mold. Wear mittens or gloves.

Build your castle on a tray, a picnic table, or a porch. To stick the ice shapes together, spray water lightly on the surfaces you want attached with a plastic spray bottle. Then hold the shapes together for about 10 seconds. The freezing weather will "cement" them together for you. Decorate your finished castle with snow and icicles.

SNOW MONSTERS

SNOW SPIDER

HINT: PUT IN BRANCHES FOR LEGS LIKE THIS AND THEN TURN THE SPIDER OVER.

SNOW DINOSAUR

STONE TEETH

Snow Monsters

When it comes to making snow monsters, just let your imagination take over. How about a giant snow snake? Or a great white shark? You can pile up mounds of snow and pack them into shapes, roll big balls of snow, or mold snow in large containers like garbage cans. Be sure to give your monster lots of personality—and that means plenty of horns, teeth, and claws. If your monster has feet, add monster tracks.

SNOW SHARK

COAT-HANGER

SMALL TIN CANS

SNOBOT: MOLD FROM A GARBAGE CAN AND SPRAY LIGHTLY WITH WATER FOR A SHINY LOOK

CARVE SLOT FOR MOUTH

COAT HANGER ARM

SNOW SNAKE

How to make monster tracks:

Cut monster footprints out of cardboard. Make holes in the footprints and loop string through the holes. Tie the footprints to your boots. Now walk up to the back of your monster.

Catch a Falling Snowflake

Did you know that every single snowflake is different from every other snowflake? If you don't believe this, catch a few flakes and see for yourself. You will need a piece of dark fabric (velvet or felt is best), a piece of cardboard about the same size, a magnifying glass, and a cold day when dry, light snow is falling.

Put the cloth on top of the cardboard to make a "snowflake catcher." Chill your snowflake catcher in the freezer before you use it so that the snowflakes won't melt as soon as they land on it. When you hold it out, try to catch only a few small snowflakes at a time. You don't need many. Then take a look at them through your magnifying glass.

Hint: The biggest snowflakes aren't the best to look at because they're just bunches of small ones stuck together.

YOU MIGHT SEE
SNOWFLAKES THAT LOOK
LIKE THESE